ALSO BY DEBORAH LARSEN

The White

Stitching Porcelain:
After Matteo Ricci in Sixteenth-Century China

The Tulip and the Pope

The Tulip
and the Pope

DEBORAH LARSEN

Alfred A. Knopf   New York   2005

THIS IS A BORZOI BOOK
PUBLISHED BY ALFRED A. KNOPF

www.aaknopf.com

Knopf, Borzoi Books, and the colophon are registered trademarks
of Random House, Inc.

Library of Congress Cataloging-in-Publication Data
Larsen, Deborah.
The tulip and the Pope / Deborah Larsen.–1st ed.
p.   cm.
ISBN 0-375-41360-X
1. Larsen, Deborah. 2. Authors, American—20th century—
Biography. 3. Catholics—United States—Biography.
4. Ex-nuns—United States—Biography. I. Title.
PS3562.A729 Z476 2005
813'.54—dc22
[B]   2004064904

Manufactured in the United States of America
First Edition

For David Cowan

Contents

CONTENTS

CONTENTS

ix

CONTENTS

CONTENTS

Author's Note

This is a work of nonfiction. But some small amount of fictionalizing seemed inevitable from the first: as a young nun (forty years ago), I kept no journal. I have invented a few details so as to make up for insufficiencies of memory; in this way I hoped to give more, not less, of a sense of things as they were.

The larger events and encounters all actually happened; the reader might want to know that in this area I made up nothing. My remembrance of 1960–1965 never felt like a conventional narrative, though it had progressions. My sense was more of a string of paper lanterns—Elaine Pagels's "*epinoia* . . . hints and glimpses, images and stories"—lit spottily against the dark along a dock, where some days, even now, waves dash.

A few persons have told me that they did not wish to be identified here (even if their words and actions would have cast them in the most favorable of lights). I have omitted some names, then, and changed others; I also occasionally altered locations, small details, and sequences of events. I did the same for those people from my past life whom I could not contact. Random initials identify some nuns because of the plethora of proper names that were (or are) actually in use in the BVM Community.

PART ONE

Becoming a Postulant

Taxi

Blue smoke curled out of the taxicab windows.

The driver, who had just parked outside what looked like a stone mansion, waited; he had most likely been through this before. Three of us, three young women, sat in his Yellow Cab and smoked our cigarettes.

The mansion was the Motherhouse of the Sisters of Charity of the Blessed Virgin Mary. And this day, July 31, 1960, was Entrance Day, the day we would give our lives to God by joining the convent. About two weeks earlier, on the anniversary of the storming of the Bastille, on July 14, I had celebrated my nineteenth birthday.

Other taxicabs were pulling into the motherhouse like limousines to the Oscar awards or like horses to the Bar X corral. One hundred and eighteen of us wanted to become nuns.

Many of us were edgy and sat smoking and speculating a little, like starlets or cowpunchers before it was time to crush out the cigarettes or flick them away and do the next things that needed to be done.

Edgy, yes, we were—but also blithe to become nuns, just as Thomas More had been blithe to bare his neck and have his head neatly sliced off by the likes of the black-hooded executioner in *A Man for All Seasons*. Thomas was so chipper because he knew he was headed for God, would see God face-to-face. Robert Bolt has Thomas say—or maybe Thomas said it himself—that God "will not refuse one who is so blithe to go to him."

In a way, we were going to Him now.

I was going to Him now. When I died, why would He refuse me if I had been a good nun? It was quite a bit like being a princess; eventually I would come into my own and inherit the transfigured earth and the kingdom of heaven.

Maybe the Yellow Cab driver, unless he was Catholic, actually did think he was my executioner. I would give him a big tip, all the money I had left, and I would give him the rest of my cigarettes.

The motherhouse, the convent of wine-colored stone, looked huge as a Cotswold manor house or an estate in Croton-on-Hudson. But the river at the base of the bluffs on which this building stood was the Mississippi, as it flowed past the southern edge of the city of Dubuque, Iowa.

In 1960 most of us didn't know much about the path of the Mississippi or the life on it or where the bluffs began or ended. Did the river mostly remind us of the flux of all things, or even of Jim and Huck? It did not. It might have been the Tiber or the Loire, the Tigris, the Ruhr, or the Yangtze. No matter. What we wanted that day was to become nuns.

We didn't give a fig about our position in the landscape.

Smoke

My friends Teresa (Tessa) and Kathleen (Kathy) and I thought of ourselves as savvy. We knew what to do because another friend's sister, who was already a nun in the order we were joining, had told us the tradition. On Entrance Day we were to give our last cigarettes to the cabdriver.

We three had come in the Yellow Cab across a bridge over the river, from the train station in East Dubuque, Illinois. We had gotten on that train at Union Station in Saint Paul, Minnesota—our hometown.

Twelve young women in all had come from Minnesota to be nuns, but I knew Tessa and Kathy the best. I had been friends with Tessa since we were both about five years old. She had lovely black hair and an interesting, angular face and white teeth; some of her relatives had been actors; she was talented in art and she spoke her mind in an honest way. Kathy came from a large family and had brown hair; her eyes and her mouth worked together when she smiled, and we always felt we could trust her and her kindness.

A letter from what would be our new community had earlier asked that our parents please not drive us to Dubuque. The Sisters wanted to avoid what could always threaten to turn into weeping and the gnashing of teeth at their gates.

Just watch your daughter disappear through the doors of a convent. Try looking down at her feet in black flats walking away from you into the religious life. Better to put her on the train, the Burlington Northern, so that it felt like she was going off to college.

I sat in that cab and smoked two cigarettes at a time.

To be funny.

I thought I was being funny, trying to look frantic to smoke them all up, juggling the two lit cigarettes, Kents, in my ringless fingers. In the end, I would still have plenty of cigarettes left for my taxi driver, who undoubtedly watched us through his rear-view mirror. I felt like a comedian.

We had smoked since freshman year in our all-girls Catholic high school, which was called Our Lady of Peace. We certainly weren't allowed to smoke at Our Lady of Peace. But after school some of the bolder of us—not I—would walk a couple of blocks down Victoria Street to, say, Grand Avenue and step into their boyfriends' '55 Oldsmobile 98s or '56 Chevrolets (which action was also not allowed by our school), and within thirty seconds the smoking started. Off they went, Bernadette inhaling, Tom exhaling; Patricia blowing smoke through her nose, Mark grasping the knob on his steering wheel to make a dashing left turn, a louie.

We had been instructed to bring only enough money to get us to the convent, and I must have tried to calculate it before I left home, which was on Goodrich Avenue in Saint Paul: so much for a ham sandwich and a Coke on the train, and maybe a Nut Goodie or a Mounds bar; so much for cab fare and tip—that was it.

And so we handed over that cab fare and that tip and the rest of our cigarettes, and that part was over. The cabdriver thanked us.

We thanked him. It was time, just the way it was "time" when the curtain went up in the high school plays in which we had acted. *Mother Was a Freshman. The Song of Bernadette. The Little World of Don Camillo.*

"It's time, girls."

We stopped laughing, got out of the cab, and walked up the sidewalk.

Several Sisters were at the door to welcome us. Even before I stepped over the threshold I felt relief from the heat. The motherhouse, I thought, was going to feel good compared to the muggy Iowa summer afternoon.

I had seen the motherhouse before but I had never been inside.

But Why

I had seen the motherhouse, Mount Carmel, because I had lived in Dubuque while I attended Clarke College for a year before I entered the convent. Some of my friends and I had driven across town to look around the convent grounds.

"What about waiting a year?" my parents had finally said when I told them I wanted to become a nun right after high school.

They had not stopped and stared; they had not winced; they had not blinked—although one time after I had sat holding one of my sister Judy's newborns, my mother said, "I saw you looking at that baby."

They just said, "Fine. But what about waiting a year?"

In the end, I waited and went to college for the academic year 1959–1960.

No one asked me why I wanted to be a nun. No one needed to ask, except the young Protestant couple who lived next door. I hadn't known many Protestants, but I loved this couple.

"But why do you want to be a nun?" they would ask. (They, like most of us, had never heard of the older distinction between a Sister and a nun; the latter belonged to what was called a contemplative order, and was cloistered.) From the screened porch where they sat drinking Old-Fashioneds before dinner, they had watched me go out on date after date.

I would sigh.

Would Protestants understand how much you loved God? Could you speak to them about such a thing without their getting embarrassed?

Bashful

I loved God. Maybe I could have spoken to my neighbors in the language of the parts of scripture I loved best. In this way, it wouldn't have sounded just like *me*. For I was bashful. I didn't want to sound like myself—who was *I*, anyway?—or like some sentimental dope.

What other language did I have, really, besides the one that had been handed to me by the Church and the scriptures? The only ideas I had about God—the Father, the Son, and the Holy Ghost—would have come from tradition, from authority. It was important in those days that the words be sanctioned so I didn't end up sounding bizarre or, worse, heretical, like the Arians, the Gnostics, or those southern French Albigensians who had been exterminated, according to the dictionary, during the Inquisition. The language of Holy Scripture, which I took to be the language of God and of the Roman Catholic Church—for the Church in a sense owned the whole Bible, I thought—was thrilling.

So if I had thought of it, I could have taken the Bible—for we had not memorized long passages in those days—and read from it to my neighbors. It would have been just like Readers' Theatre, in which I had participated in high school.

In the beginning God created heaven and earth.
And the earth was void and empty, and darkness was upon the face of the deep; and the spirit of God moved over the waters.

I would continue reading aloud about how God created a light, which He called Day, and a darkness, which He called Night;

about how the firmament came from His Hands and the creeping creatures and the great whales. The winged fowls and seeds that grew into herbs and trees would come next. And then man and woman, and the river that divided into the four heads of Phison, Gehon, Tigris, and Euphrates. I would read the part about how God brought the beasts and the fowls to Adam "to see what he would name them."

Since God wanted "to see" what Adam would name them, I would eventually decide that God was quite a curious Person. Such curiosity on His part endeared Him to me, as did His allowing mere humans to name the things of this world.

How could you not adore the Person who had done all this? He made everything. He must have been something. Why does something exist and not nothing? Easy. Someone was kind enough to create it. He dreamt things up: you would never have thought of seeds, for instance. What you couldn't do with seeds down through the ages! And herbs: he must have thought of something for healing and to flavor cooking. And Leviathan: all that baleen for straining plankton. What an imagination. Everything was absolutely original with Him, the Absolute.

You shrugged off all the cranky things God did in the Hebrew Bible—which most of us called the Old Testament in 1960—and you absolutely loved this Person, the One Whom you could just imagine moving over the waters. You wanted to live as close as you could to Him, live in His Shadow.

Why not dedicate yourself to Him as completely as you could? It was a cinch. Why didn't millions of people do this every day, like the lemmings in the Arctic who sometimes grow so restless for something that they leave home and head downhill to wherever water is and think nothing of it.

"Because," my mother would say. "Because if everyone entered religion"—in those days, in going into the convent or the monastery or the seminary, one "entered religion"—"eventually there would be no people."

I took that as a joke. Or I took it to mean that she thought that the world needed marriage in order to produce little babies who would grow up to be people.

Through the Door

I stepped across the threshold of the convent. Besides feeling the coolness, I saw, as my eyes adjusted to the low light, long halls and polished wooden floors.

"Kathy. Tessa. Debby." Someone who knew us was greeting us: a Sister from our high school who happened to be at the motherhouse that summer.

Sister W. was a smart, tall woman, youngish; she looked right at each person she addressed and had a full, kind of snorting laugh. She was pleasant but wasn't wasting any time: she said she would take a small group of us on a brief tour to see the chapel and to see where we would sleep.

I had never seen where it was that nuns slept. Not only were we getting closer to the mystery that had always surrounded the nuns; now we had actually entered that magic sphere as more than mere visitors to convent parlors.

We were in.

Counterpanes

In *The Nun's Story*, a novel based on a true story, written by Kathryn Hulme, which I had read and reread in the late 1950s, Gabrielle Van der Mal, the young Belgian nurse who entered the convent and became Sister Luke, slept on a straw sack on wooden planks at the motherhouse. But I knew, as my mother would say, that that was "medieval"—a word she used in a number of contexts.

Monica Baldwin, British, in her 1949 nonfiction work, *I Leap over the Wall*, writes that the woolen sheets on the nuns' beds were washed just once a year. Also medieval.

Here was my modern reality: the inside of a small dormitory. Each room's door had above it a sign imprinted with a saint's name: "Saint Roche" or "Saint Anne" or "Saint Jude" or "Saint Polycarp."

I would sleep in this last—"Saint Polycarp." During the time of Marcus Aurelius, Polycarp, the bishop of Smyrna, had been burned alive because of his Christian faith; we celebrated his feast day and martyrdom at Mass every January 26. The name of my high school study hall proctor had been Sister Mary Polycarp.

There were six iron beds with white bedspreads on them. They had regular mattresses on exposed springs. As in a ward in a hospital, steel poles seemed to run everywhere, and to them were attached heavy curtains on pull rings: looking like unbleached muslin or hemp, these curtains were pleated and neatly fastened with a cotton tie to a pole at one side of each bed. The floors were wooden; the windows' dark shutters were open. Next to each bed was a small dresser with a white dresser scarf on it: on this rested a washbasin, a pitcher, and a plastic glass. A simple chair sat in each of the six little alcoves.

My bed, Sister W. indicated, was the first on the left, next to the door.

I looked at what would become my bed.

I thought: *Well.*

Everything was neat and perfectly clean. The six identical small beds were covered with snow white counterpanes.

Not seven little beds.

§

But the seventh when he looked at his bed saw little Snow White, who was lying asleep therein. And he called the others, who came running up, and they cried out with astonishment, and brought their seven little candles and let the light fall on little Snow White. "Oh, heavens! oh heavens!" cried they, "what a lovely child!" and they were so glad that they did not wake her up but let her sleep on in the bed.

The Chapel

Sister W. took our little group into the chapel for a few minutes. She smiled at us and indicated what we should do by taking the lead, moving forward to one of the back pews, genuflecting, slipping into it, and kneeling down.

The pews (unlike those in my parish church at home, Saint Luke's, a massive structure at the corner of Lexington and Summit Avenues in Saint Paul) were short, truncated somehow, meant for two. They were of blond wood.

Here was the altar, above which was a huge crucifix; here was the hanging red sanctuary lamp; here were the two side altars—one with a statue of Saint Joseph and one with a statue of Mary. Here on the main altar were the beeswax candles and the flowers—and the tabernacle itself. There were the fourteen Stations of the Cross, and there were the stained-glass windows.

Although God was everywhere, He was fully present in this tabernacle under the form of bread. The lit sanctuary lamp let me know that He was there, that the reserved Blessed Sacrament, consecrated at Mass this morning, was there.

If He was there, I felt, what else did I need? This place, this chapel where I would become a nun: even though I had not been here before, I had been here before.

I had always been there, in a church, in a chapel; I had been in these places for as long as I could remember. I had been there since my first conscious view of my mother removing her white cotton gloves in church before the beginning of Sunday Mass at Saint Luke's. I was small, but not too small to have my own white gloves.

I had my own missal, too. Mother was an expert in navigating her missal. Even when I was too young to grasp the book's contents, she set the ribbon markers at the right spots for me before Mass began. When she, at the right moment in the service, grasped the yellow ribbed marker and flipped a chunk of her tissue-paper-thin pages so that she arrived at the Introit prayer for that Sunday, I grasped my ribbon, and *flip* went my chunk, too.

Mother's fingers, with their nails painted Red-Hot Red, rested on the page. When the priest had finished reading the Introit verses for that particular Sunday—say, *"Exsurge, quare obdormis, Domine?"* and so on—*flip* went her pages by way of a celery-colored ribbon, and *flip* went my pages. We were both back at the place where the Mass's parts remained the same from Sunday to Sunday.

The pages smelled good. Mother smelled good. If it was a

High Mass, even more solemn than most Masses, the incense smelled, if not good, interesting.

I knew the smell of incense as well as I would later know the Tabu or the Evening in Paris that as a young woman I used to squirt or splash all over myself so I could smell good-and-sophisticated.

"My father likes you; but he says you wear too much perfume," one of my boyfriends, Leo, had said. The father smoked—always, it seemed—a pipe, and the tobacco he used had a potent, not unattractive fragrance.

"He does?" Uh-oh, I thought. The father, a psychiatrist, must be right.

"And I told him," Leo said with aplomb, "I told Dad, 'Oh, that perfume? That's her way of combating the smell of your pipe.' "

The vestments, vessels, and altar cloths at Saint Luke's were also interesting, with complicated names—cassocks and surplices, albs and stoles and chasubles; not only chalices but chalice veils and palls (stiff squares of linen). I was beside myself the day I found priest and altar-boy paper dolls—with Mass vestments and vessel cutouts—for sale in a Catholic bookstore.

We loved to play Mass ourselves, although we weren't sure it was quite right. My brother, Damon, was the priest, of course—I don't remember my sister playing—and I got to be an altar boy, which would never have happened to a girl in real life. My brother was solemn and correct, neat and precise with his hands, like a real priest. We took Wonder Bread, cut the crusts off, and made round hosts from it, squishing and slapping them flat to look unleavened. We had grape juice for wine, but only the priest, Father Damon, got to drink that. We borrowed our mother's old dinner bell to ring at the consecration. I got to ring it. Not one bit of mockery lay within this: it was intense and reverent play.

I was confirmed at Saint Luke's. My sister was married there. I sometimes left the playground at the parish school and went to pray there alone, at recess, offering up my scraped palms and knees for the Poor Souls in purgatory.

As fifth-graders, we often left school as a group to go to the choir loft and sing for the funeral Masses that occurred on weekdays. The soloist would leave us shuddering when she sang out, partway through the "Dies Irae," *"Rex tremendae majestatis, qui salvandos salvas gratis."* She would sing, *"REX tremendae . . ."* Purified Wagner. Too much of an alto to shatter glass. We, the conscripted funeral Mass singers, were ten and eleven years old.

At one point in the evening Tenebrae service, during Holy Week, all lights in the church were extinguished, every single candle was snuffed out, and the regular adult choir, miles above us in their loft, took hymnbooks and banged on their pews to signify the rending of the veil of the temple at the very instant that the Lord had died. Every year I waited for this, for Tenebrae to roll around.

On Good Friday I stood in line to kneel down and kiss the feet of an alabaster Christ, affixed to the giant cross that was brought from the sanctuary to the parishioners' side of the communion rail. In some sense, by doing this, I was hoping I would make it up to Him for dying for me.

If all the world was a stage, then the inside of Saint Luke's Church was upstage center.

The chapel in the convent differed from Saint Luke's in two ways: it was smaller, more intimate, and therefore seemed like *down*-stage center; and whereas some of the art in Saint Luke's was borderline, every centimeter of the Mount Carmel chapel was elegant, in good taste.

One characteristic of the BVMs, the order I was entering, was that good taste. When I left Saint Luke's parish grade school and went to Our Lady of Peace High School, where BVMs taught, I entered a world that had a distinctly different aesthetic tinge to it.

My childhood had been filled with statues of the Infant of Prague and pictures of what was called the Sacred Heart of Jesus—Jesus' face was bland if shining, His hair long, His finger pointing to His chest, where I saw an exposed or superimposed heart, which was pierced by thorns and which dripped blood. I never set eyes on art like that at Our Lady of Peace, where every bit of the decor seemed to me to be on the modern side. A statue of the Virgin Mary, for example, had clean lines; her sculpted face radiated composure, kindness, intelligence; her nose was somewhat aristocratic.

The face of the convent's Virgin also looked benign and, as in "Silent Night," calm and bright. Now that I had come down to dwell among the BVMs, the motherhouse statuary confirmed my sense that all would be well. Mount Carmel was not only shipshape. It had style.

The Sitting Pulpit

Sister W. told us that we would go to the postulate, a room where we would gather daily. On the way down, the polished hardwood of the stairs and one landing seemed to emanate light rather than to reflect it. We followed a hall, punctuated on either side by doors to what looked like offices and classrooms, to its end and entered a huge room.

In the postulate were long tables with desk chairs neatly pushed in under them. On one wall there were small, built-in drawers, or cubbies, which would contain sewing supplies for mending clothes.

The tables faced a low, enclosed sort of sitting pulpit with a little door on the side of it. This would be the pulpit from which the Mistress of Postulants, Sister C., would give what were called "Instructions."

Later, when the Postulant Mistress sat in this structure, we could see her only from about her diaphragm up to the top of her hooded head. Though getting into it (I think there was a stair or two) required no side ladder with red manropes and mahogany-stained foot pieces, and though Sister C. would never cry out, "Starboard gangway there!" that strange sitting pulpit reminded me of the one from which Father Mapple preached in *Moby-Dick,* the one Melville calls "a self-containing stronghold."

The postulate pulpit was where, also as in Melville, "the God of breezes fair or foul is first invoked for favorable winds." The postulancy was for us a "ship on its passage out"—or in—"and not a voyage complete." The pulpit was its prow.

We understood that the voyage would be marked by months and then years, all carefully planned. First, we would be postulants for six months.

The word "postulant" had a medieval Latin root—*postulare,* a word that could have several meanings: to request, to presume, to assume without proof, to assert, to make claim for, demand, or take for granted. As a noun "postulate" can signify some basic element, underlying principle; a requirement, a prerequisite; in mathematics, an axiom.

Finally, a postulant was a petitioner, someone who was a candidate for admission into a religious order.

That's what I would be. Presumed innocent and almost a nun. Presumed almost a nun by the congregation, I assumed. They would be studying me.

Would I be studying *them*? Why would I do such a thing?

After the postulancy was over, we would don the full dress of nuns—habits—including white veils. In this state we would spend two years being novices.

Then we would make vows—of poverty, chastity, and

obedience—receive the black veil, and become professed Sisters. The vows would be temporary for the first five years; they would be pronounced by the individual Sister during Mass on February 2 and they would be renewed on February 2 of the following year unless, of course, someone left, which was unthinkable.

After five years came permanent vows, the "I vow to Thee . . . for *one year*" being replaced by the "I vow to Thee . . . *forever.*" If someone left the convent after making permanent vows, even more unthinkable, she would have to be dispensed from them by Rome, that is, by the Pope, via the curial department called the Sacred Congregation for Religious.

Seclusion characterized the postulancy and novitiate: it was an essentially cloistered existence and it would be spent at Mount Carmel. After taking vows, we would step out into the world by continuing our education at one of the community's two colleges or—for those who already had degrees—by being "missioned" to teach at one of the BVM elementary or secondary schools, which were located all over the United States. Each BVM school had a convent attached to or near it, so we would live in common as we had done at the motherhouse; we would have Mass together, eat together, pray together, have recreation periods together.

Most of our "set," the Set of 1960, had arrived by now—it was late afternoon—and Sister C. rang a little bell from the prow of her ship and indicated that we could sit down at the long tables. I had become separated from Tessa and Kathy in the flurry of meeting other young women.

Sister C. smiled and her china pink cheeks plumped up. Her fingers hung over the wood of the pulpit: those of us who were close to the front could see that her fingernails were short, but not too short, not bitten; they were perfectly rounded, immaculate. The fingernails' half-moons showed; the cuticles must have been carefully pushed back with an orangewood stick.

Tomorrow, she told us, we would become postulants, putting on for the first time the black serge skirts, blouses, and capes we had brought, had packed into our black metal trunks. Some of us had sewn these garments ourselves or had asked one of our high school nun teachers to sew them. I had mine made for me. Any sewing that I ever did ended in what was the equivalent of a fallen cheese soufflé.

Finally, we were given little cards that said, in my case, "Welcome, Deborah, to our Convent and your new home! It's a large one, so this will help you find your way around."

Assignments followed, cast in terms of numbers: I was to sit in a certain spot at a certain postulate table. I received a community number, 4,000-something, which I would stitch on all clothing that would be laundered. My compartment, or cubby, in the postulate had yet another number. My table in the refectory had a number and I was to sit in a particular chair. I was assigned to a certain pew in a certain row in the chapel, and to a certain bed (number 1) in a certain dormitory on a certain floor. It seemed like summer camp, or maybe the military.

Listening to what we would do next and what after that and what after that, I was distracted for a moment—I became aware that I wanted something. What?

I wanted to have a cigarette.

Opening the cigarette package had been a ritual. Anticipating your cigarette, you grasped the tiny leader strip ribbon and pulled it all around until the cellophane separated. Then you opened only one small section of the foil casing so that the tops of just a few cigarettes would lie exposed. You were careful, extracting one tobacco-filled cylinder with the tips of the fingernails of your thumb and index finger. You liked not denting the filter tip.

There were no cigarettes in the postulate, however, and without having smoked I went downstairs with the other young women, where I saw for the first time where nuns ate: the refectory.

The Refectory

The convent refectory was a huge room with wooden floors and long tables that seated ten persons. We had been told that when we went down to eat, we should stand at our places behind the chairs and wait in silence until everyone was assembled, grace said, and a bell rung. Then we could be seated, but should still be silent until the little bell was rung the second time. Then we could speak.

This was not exceptional. I was more than used, from Catholic school, to filing into a place in perfect silence.

The tables were covered with oilcloth of a light green color. The place settings were as I had been taught to arrange them: fork to the left of the plate; knife to the right, blade turned in toward the plate; and spoon on the far right, with a cup and saucer next to it. A glass of water sat at the tip of the knife.

A "professed Sister," one who had taken vows, sat at the head of each table. We all talked at this, our first supper. The Sister asked us to introduce ourselves, to tell from where we had come.

The conversation at my table was restrained but pleasant. No one was crying. Meanwhile, white-veiled novices began serving us family-style, handing the platters or bowls to the head of our table.

Out of disorientation and excitement, I did not pay much attention to the food, which consisted of thick-crusted, home-made white bread and cold cuts and applesauce. It was clearly a supper and not the kind of dinner I ate at home.

We did the dishes at the table after we ate, bringing large pans of soapy water and rinse water and drying towels from the convent kitchen. Summer camp again. Only, the time surrounding summer-camp dish doing was boisterous and the first convent dish doing was silent.

I was on the lookout for someone doing penance in the refectory, as my heroine from Hulme's novel had done. Sister Luke, this sophisticated and well-educated young woman, had gone from nun to nun after all had started eating and, on her knees, silently begged for two spoonfuls of soup from each of her Sisters' bowls.

I saw nothing of the sort. My mother was right. Indeed, I had chosen a progressive, modern order; I had not chosen a medieval one. The BVMs looked like the avant-garde up against those Old World nuns. I felt pretty smug.

And perhaps just the slightest bit disappointed.

Us

There were ten people at each refectory table and one of them was a professed Sister; our set filled about thirteen tables. We were mostly from the Midwest and the West.

We were from Iowa (Clinton, Des Moines, Dubuque, Bellevue, Waterloo, Emmitsburg, Fort Dodge, Panora, West Liberty, Farley). We were from Washington (Seattle); we were from Arizona (Phoenix, Cottonwood); we were from Minnesota (Saint Paul, Lake Elmo, Duluth).

We came from Kansas (Wichita) and from California (North

Hollywood, La Crescenta, Petaluma, Glendale, Burbank, Tujunga, and Sunland). And from Montana: Missoula and Butte.

Those of us from Illinois had been residents of Chicago, Wilmette, Long Lake, Rock Island, Grayslake, Cicero, and Skokie. The Missourians were from Saint Louis; the Nebraskans were from Omaha and Lincoln.

Berlin, Sister Bay, and Milwaukee were the Wisconsin towns from which we came. Finally, one of us came from Gillette, Wyoming; one from South Bend, Indiana; another from Kilauea, Hawaii; one more from Rapid City, South Dakota; another from Cincinnati, Ohio.

I liked it that these young women were from all over. I liked the sounds of the names of their hometowns. It made things seem cosmopolitan.

We looked, I thought, for the most part healthy and attractive—a few were downright beautiful—and young, of course. We ranged in age from about eighteen to about twenty-one; some of us were right out of high school; some of us had been to a year or two of college; some of us had just earned bachelor's degrees. A few of us came from wealthy or from poor backgrounds, but most of us came from hardworking middle-class families.

Our hair shone. Our eyes shone. Most of us were not long out of the womb.

The next day we would pack away in our trunks the clothing we had worn to the convent—the blackwatch plaid shirtdress, the blue-and-white-striped gathered skirt, the seersucker blouse. These vestiges of our lives in the world would be kept until we took our vows and then they would be discarded.

We had already given away our heavier clothing and our jewelry to our younger sisters or to cousins or friends—the cashmere or Orlon sweater sets, the wool jumpers, the long strings of pop-it beads, the camel coats, the ankle bracelets.

We were the true blonds, the dishwater blonds, the peroxide

blonds that would grow out; the auburns, the reds; light browns, dark browns; the matte jet blacks and the glossy blacks. We were the curly-headed, the pixies, the pageboys, the straight-banged, and we even had one—did she really want to become a nun? I thought—ducktail. In the late 1950s, we saw someone who wore a ducktail as a hood. One syllable away from a hoodlum.

Which one was *I*? I was the one from Saint Paul who described my own hair to myself as an affliction since it was naturally curly and so decidedly not stylish in the fifties. I kept it cut but still it waved in its shortness and made me look, I thought, like a failed imitation of a flapper. I longed to have hair that would swing easily into a perfect pageboy—like Rosemary Clooney's—as I rose from my bed in the morning.

Besides the awful curl in it, my poor hair was losing its light color. I had scrutinized it in the mirror at home and at college as the months of '59 and '60 passed. Now it could fairly be called that sad shade, dishwater blond.

Most of us didn't have a sense of just how carefully we had been examined by the Sisters of Charity. We would later find out what the BVM Constitutions had to say:

ADMISSION TO THE CONGREGATION

Every young Catholic woman who is not debarred by any legitimate impediment and is inspired by a right intention and is fit to bear the burdens of the religious life can be admitted into the Congregation.

For the admission of Postulants the permission of the provincial Superior is required and sufficient.

Prudence demands that the greatest care should be exercised in the admission of those who ask to enter our Congregation. Each applicant must present before admission certificates of Baptism and Confirmation; from her pastor or from another priest who knows her well, written testimonials regarding her moral character, her state of freedom, and the uprightness of her family; also a testimonial from a doctor regarding her sufficiency of health.

With the consent of the Superior General and the deliberative vote of the General Council the following may be admitted for a just and reasonable cause:

1. those who are over thirty years of age
2. widows
3. illegitimates who have not been duly legitimated.

Invalidly admitted to the Novitiate are those

1. who after having abandoned the Catholic faith joined some non-Catholic or atheistic sect
2. who have not attained the age requisite for the novitiate
3. who are bound by matrimony
4. who are or have been bound by religious vows
5. who are threatened with punishment for the commission of a grave crime of which they have been or can be accused
6. who enter religion under the influence of violence, grave fear, or fraud; also those whom the Superior receives under pressure of the same influence.

Safe to say that we, in our late teens and early twenties, would not be invalidly admitted. We had not had time to flee marriages, commit a grave crime, embrace atheism, bounce from convent to convent, or otherwise misrepresent ourselves. Why in the world would women who had done these things want to be nuns anyway?

That first night, I had not a real sense of any of my new companions as individuals. But I was comforted by their presence, by their general good will. However mixed some of our motives may have been, as a group we fairly pulsed with idealism and purpose. We had all come to give our lives to God.

We did not think that what we were doing was one bit odd.

The Clothing List

After supper we unpacked our suitcases and some of us went to All Saints, the provision storeroom, to bring clothing up to our alcoves. Before we entered the convent, each one of us had received a clothing list.

In reading this list and in buying items from it, some of us felt like voyeurs. This was our initiation into what nuns wore, even what they wore right up against their skin, against unmentionable parts. It seemed creepy. We wondered, without a shred of irony, whether we really wanted to know *this* much about nuns. (Someone had told me that in earlier ages, nuns, for the sake of total modesty, took baths with their clothes on, and I thought that odd but somehow appropriate, understandable, and what's more, clever of them.)

Some of the items to be brought in suitcase and trunk:

3 blouses in an approved style
2 black skirts
2 black underskirts
6 T-shirts (short-sleeved)
6 pairs cotton pants
2 girdles
3 bras
8 pairs full-length black hosiery

2 pairs black oxfords with military or cuban heels—*soft*
   rubber heels added
2 pair white summer pajamas
Plain black night slippers (with soft soles and heels)
Black robe (full-length)
1 dozen white handkerchiefs
1 pair tennis shoes
1 black sleeveless sweater, waist length, for indoor wear
1 heavy sweater for outdoor wear
1 black skap
1 pair black mittens or gloves
1 pair boots
1 coat

We were also to bring things like soap (not highly scented), a small stand-up mirror, combs, deodorant, toothbrush, toothpaste, missal and rosary, sewing supplies (including a darning egg), black shoelaces, school supplies, stationery supplies, and personal medication.

I looked at the list. A *skap* sounded ominous. What was it, some kind of conventual torture device, or maybe a chastity belt? It turned out to be only a combination hat and scarf for winter.

Bras. What to think? Well. OK.

Bring girdles to the convent? Strange. Maybe girdles with garters so that we could hold up those long black stockings?

For all the bras and girdles and pants, there was no mention of bringing Kotex or Modess or sanitary belts. I supposed that the Sisters could not bring themselves to this, to listing the things that touched so starkly on bodily functions. Better to supply them at the convent.

I noticed that there was no watch on the list. Watches and clocks were not permitted as personal items during the two-and-one-half-year training period. We could wear our present glasses during the first six months, but when we became novices they would be changed (recut?) to semihexagonal lenses with white-gold rimless frames. We were warned, though, that if we had narrow lenses such as the "harlequin style," these would give unsatisfactory vision when the plastic frames were removed. Better to go right to new glasses with rimless frames before we came.

At the convent we would receive white collars and military-style capes, split in front. And we would later receive our "blues"—light denim capes and aprons for domestic work like peeling vegetables, working in the Bake House, scrubbing bathrooms, dusting parlors. The only veils we would have in those months were tiny square ones that we plopped on top of our heads when we went to chapel.

The clothing list included names of firms from which we could order catalogs and from which we could purchase certain items:

Cabrini House
552 Mission Street
San Francisco 5, California

FitzPatrick, Inc.
62 Murray Street
New York 7, New York

Cora Geis Convent Hosiery
P.O. Box 806
Milwaukee 1, Wisconsin

Jamieson
1006 S. Michigan Boulevard
Chicago 5, Illinois

McCosker, Inc.
129 Duane Street
New York 13, New York

I ordered my own things from Cora Geis and from Jamie-
son, in Milwaukee and in Chicago. I had actually visited both
Milwaukee and Chicago several times. I had been all over the
Midwest.

A statement about financial arrangements also accompanied
the list. We were to bring a dowry of $50. Canon law—Church
law—specified that this dowry could not be omitted. After I took
my first vows, the dowry would be invested in "safe, lawful, and
productive" securities, and never actually be expended until I
died. If I left the convent, the dowry would be returned to me,
minus any interest.

We or our parents were to provide the community with $25 a
month for board and tuition for thirty months—this was to help
with apparel or other supplies that might be needed.

The list's style and its tone were quite matter-of-fact. A literate ship's purser might have written those pages.

The Cape

That first evening we were issued capes and we hung these along
with our new black blouses and skirts on hangers on one of the
steel poles that marked our sleeping spaces. We were also given
white collars.

These collars were semistiff bands that attached to the capes.
I liked the collars: they reminded me of the Roman collars that
priests wore. They would lend authority. In fact, the very next

day they would lend that authority because we would be wearing them.

In what had been my copy of *The Nun's Story,* Gabrielle as a postulant had also worn a short black cape. I knew the descriptive sentence, the opening sentence of the novel, by heart: "The short black cape hooked at the neck and dropped without flare to the middle of the forearms."

Perfect. Just like my new cape. And what a fine sentence Kathryn Hulme had written. I would put on the cape as I had somehow put on that sentence, or rather had ingested it.

> The short black cape
> > hooked
> > at the neck
> and dropped without flare to the middle of the forearms.

The words of that sentence were functional and beautiful. They were a life to be entered or breathed or swallowed, lived.

But they were no longer to be physically gazed upon in the exact book in which I had first read them. For we were not allowed to bring any of our books from home to the convent.

I thought nothing of it. Or thought I thought nothing of it.

Surely you can do without your very own books for the rest of your life, can't you?

You can do without the ones you fall asleep with, the ones that smell like a pulp mill or like mildew or the ones that smell like Belgian linen. You can do without turning to find that glittering passage—about scribblers or snow globes or an opaline sky or an enchanting force of nature that made a woman the Pope in her own right—just where you know you'll find it, on a right-hand page three-fourths of the way down or on a left-hand page near the top.

Because you were taught in school never to mar your books

by making marks in them and because you were mostly obedient, you took a mental photo of the page where your beloved passage lay.

❧

Like most young scribblers, she went abroad for her characters, and scenery; and banditti, counts, gypsies, nuns, and duchesses appeared upon her stage, and played their parts with as much accuracy and spirit as could be expected.

❧

An object his mother used as a paperweight stood beside the inkwell: a small glass sphere, on a black plastic pedestal, containing a snowman wearing a stove pipe hat. Zooey picked it up, gave it a shake, and sat apparently watching the snowflakes swirl.

❧

The Ojibways called it Oskibugi Sipi, the Young Leaf River, for on its banks the trees bud early. . . . The Dakotas called it Minisota, the Sky-tinted Water, for it has a look like a sky made opaline by clouds. . . . The Frenchmen called it the St. Pierre.

❧

"Husband," said she, "why are you standing there? Now, I am Emperor, but I will be Pope, too; go to the Flounder." "Alas, wife," said the man, "what will you not wish for? You cannot be Pope; there is but one in Christendom; he cannot make you Pope." "Husband," said she, "I will be Pope; go immediately, I must be Pope this very day." "No, wife," said the man, "I do

not like to say that to him; that would not do; it is too much, the Flounder can't make you Pope." "Husband," said she, "what nonsense! If he can make an emperor he can make a pope. Go to him directly. I am Emperor, and you are nothing but my husband; will you go at once?"

Then he was afraid and went; but he was quite faint and shivered and shook, and his knees and legs trembled. And a high wind blew over the land, and the clouds flew, and towards evening all grew dark, and the leaves fell from the trees, and the water rose and roared as if it were boiling, and splashed upon the shore; and in the distance he saw ships which were firing guns in their sore need, pitching and tossing on the waves. And yet in the midst of the sky there was a small bit of blue, though on every side it was as red as in a heavy storm. So, full of despair, he went and stood in much fear and said,

> "Flounder, flounder in the sea,
> Come, I pray thee, here to me;
> For my wife, good Ilsabil,
> Wills not as I'd have her will."

"Well, what does she want, then?" said the Flounder. "Alas," said the man, "she wants to be Pope." "Go to her then," said the Flounder; "she is Pope already."

So he went and when he got there, he saw what seemed to be a large church surrounded by palaces. He pushed his way through the crowd. Inside, however, everything was lighted up with thousands and thousands of candles and his wife was clad in gold . . . and all the emperors and kings were on their knees before her, kissing her shoe. "Wife," said the man, and looked attentively at her, "are you now Pope?" "Yes," said she, "I am Pope." So he stood and looked at her, and it was just as if he was looking at the bright sun. When he had stood looking at her thus for a short time, he said, "Ah, wife, if you are Pope, do *let well enough alone!" But she looked as stiff as a post, and did not move or show any signs of life. Then he said, "Wife, now that you are Pope, be satisfied, you cannot become anything greater now." "I will consider about that," said the woman. Thereupon they both went to bed. . . .*

Rustlings

Not one cigarette to be seen anywhere. Did no one think, I wondered, to have some there in case of emergency, in case some poor postulant needed just *one*? Why was it so hard to stop smoking? It felt funny, painful, as if part of my body had gone someplace and I needed to find it fast and reattach it. What I was feeling must be my fault. I had read somewhere that if you couldn't stop smoking, it meant that you had a weak character.

The first night, before we went to bed, we joined the Sisters for evening prayer and then we left the chapel with anticipation. We were going to go to our new little beds in silence.

From the very beginning we observed silence at night although we had not yet begun the formal study of the reasons behind this discipline. I went to my room, Saint Polycarp, untied the tie of my curtains, and pulled them, the steel rings rattling on the poles, around my bed. It was my little nook, my new bedroom, about eight feet by nine feet.

Sister C. had explained how we were to wash and get ready for bed.

I undressed, folded my clothes, and put them away in a drawer. No need to hang them, I thought—unfazed—as I will later on simply be taking them down to my trunk, never to put them on again. It was fun putting on the white pajamas: I had always loved new clothes. But the black bathrobe felt flimsy.

I picked up my enamel basin and cup, left the room, and went downstairs to the large bathroom to which I was assigned. It had four toilet stalls, several showers, and two sinks. I filled the basin and cup and took them back to my curtained alcove.

A washcloth and a towel hung on a little rack on one side of the dresser. I washed my face with the soap from a soap dish I would keep in the top drawer. I rinsed. Then, dampening the toothbrush, I brushed my teeth, spitting (quietly) into the used water in the basin, which I eventually carried back to the bathroom for emptying, rinsing, and refilling for the next morning so that no time would be wasted at 5 a.m.

Everyone else did the same things I did. I heard rustlings and faint spittings and bumping of basins from behind curtains that looked just like mine. Summer camp, except here there were no outhouses and here there was silence in place of talk.

My alcove was at the end of the room near the door and so the light switch, when I pulled the curtains, fell under my control. I would learn to wait until all of the rustlings and drawer closings and openings stopped, and then I would turn out the light.

Silence eventually came. I turned out the light, got into bed, and there I was. I had entered the convent.

The first night had been interesting. We were going to look like real postulants tomorrow; well, we were actually going to become postulants tomorrow. If I could just have had one cigarette before I went to sleep.

You had gone to bed without the comfort of speaking with anyone in those intimate hours before bedtime, without the comfort of a hug or a good-night kiss. Those physical delights would no longer be yours.

This was not the kind of life where you were to look back. You were headed toward becoming an empty vessel filled by the

Lord. Think, scripture said, of the things that are above, or on high, and not of the things that are below. Below meant the physical and earthiness and murk and the cravings of the flesh, and above meant the things of the spirit: there was an impermeable membrane between the two.

Besides, why would you deserve comfort before bedtime, anyway? Who really needed it?

But Why, Again

Besides loving God in 1960, I had contemplated my life choices and they appeared to be to get married or to become a spinster. My experience of mature single women was limited, whereas I had observed many married couples.

One older single relative lived alone, working as a secretary at the veterans' hospital in Saint Paul. Two friends of my mother's, one a teacher and one a social worker, did live together in an apartment. I noticed that they shared a bedroom that had twin beds in it. Couldn't they afford a two-bedroom apartment? This setup looked to me like something meant for two sisters, two little girls, rather than for grown-ups.

I knew a little of one single woman who had a career; she was a professor in New York and was also connected somehow with UNICEF. But her life seemed foreign and unattainable; she may as well have been living in a yurt among the Mongols as in her East Coast Manhattan brownstone. Even "brownstone" was new to me; it was not a term I had ever heard used in Saint Paul. I liked the compound word and I was happy to learn that a mere brown stone was not being signified. A brownstone in Manhattan. I had just begun to imagine some things about New York.

Another single relative I knew well was a nun, my maternal aunt Cleopha, who was now Sister Mary Cleopha. Here was something a little different. She was smart and focused; she had risen to the top of her order to become the Mother General of the Racine Dominicans. She knew finance; she acquired land and buildings for a college; the order grew under her care. She was determined, inflexible at times, and admired by many. But she was not a spinster; she was a nun.

And there was marriage. I knew no one in Saint Paul who was divorced, which might have made me think that there was happiness all around, but there was not happiness all around. When married couples weren't fighting they looked mostly dull or dolorous to me.

That there were some exceptions to these dismal unions struck me one day when I had been playing at my friend Tessa's house. I heard singing: it was her father, Mr. C., standing at the bottom of the staircase.

He was serenading his wife, Margaret, who was upstairs doing something. He was singing, "Peg o' my heart, I *love* you." I thought this was jolly and sweet, if corny and somewhat eccentric for a mature man.

Later I would read about Saul Bellow's aged Menasha, who rises on his toes graveside in a cemetery and sings "In questa tomba oscura," from *Aïda*, and then the spiritual "Goin' Home." Menasha's face had been turned up as he sang. He almost crowed with emotion and excitement—just as Mr. C. had almost done.

I had to admit that my sister and brother-in-law appeared happy. And that young couple next door to me, the ones who asked all the questions, did seem pretty joyful and lively; they played tennis together. But they didn't quite count because they were Protestant and hadn't been married in the Catholic Church.

But my own mother and father? I didn't even want to think

about it. Too complicated. Too complicated because I saw them both loving each other and suffering each other as well as suffering from certain events.

My father was born in 1903. He became a banker, who along with his father and grandfather had owned and operated the sole bank in New Prague, Minnesota. Before his marriage he had lived as a kind of country gentleman. He worked hard, but he loved to fish. He played a silver flute in a small dance band. He and his friends outwitted the authorities time after time as they ran whiskey across the Canadian border into northern Minnesota during Prohibition. He played tennis and he golfed: his family built their own tennis court as well as a nine-hole golf course.

Then came the stock market crash of 1929, the Great Depression, and the bank holiday of 1933. My father's family's fortunes were on the wane. By this time he had met my mother, who had come from Marquette, where she had been working on a master's degree, to teach high school in New Prague. Now the country gentleman and his fiancée had to elope to Duluth to get married for lack of money for a wedding.

The fiancée, born in 1904, had not been a country girl at all; she was thoroughly citified, having grown up as the daughter of Michael Peil, a wholesale grocer, and Mary Peil, a socialite who knew how to get power in those days in a largely Catholic Saint Paul by cultivating the clergy, including the archbishop. After my grandmother died, my mother and her father lived in the Commodore Hotel in Saint Paul at the same time that F. Scott Fitzgerald did.

But now my newly married parents had slipped out of a moneyed Jazz Age into a decade where they were fairly poor. My father drank heavily; they argued over this. My mother developed multiple fears—of cats, dogs, airplanes; of my father driving more than twenty-five miles an hour; of pregnancy. Using the only means of birth control available to them as Roman

Catholics, the rhythm method, meant that in 1941 they had produced me.

Once in a while, it was true that I would see them standing quietly in a hallway with their arms around each other. But that didn't seem to me to have enough redeeming value in it.

All in all, I figured marriage was, at best, pretty spotty.

And of course, married people functioned as parents. Procreation was one of the big ends of marriage. Most everyone had children. My parents told of one couple who had not had children because they were essentially selfish people. Somehow this pair ended up bedridden at fairly young ages and the unspoken idea was that either this was a punishment or, at the very least, it served them right.

The mothers darned socks with black darning eggs and served up corned beef hash out of cans and vacuumed and ironed men's handkerchiefs and daughters' pink hair ribbons. In the wickedly hot Saint Paul summers they tried to keep their babies cool and free of heat rash and they themselves wore sleeveless dresses with rickrack at the necklines. Backyard zinnias and marigolds flourished under their hands. They served Russian salads for supper at card tables set up on screened porches. They went to College Club luncheons and to Como Park for picnics and they silently, anxiously practiced the rhythm method and went to church on Sundays with artificial cherries and short face veils attached to their brimmed hats. They had highballs with their husbands after five o'clock. Was it after the highballs, later that night, that the rhythm method fell apart?

The fathers worked for businesses like triple-A and 3M and Northern States Envelope Company. They wore hats and white shirts and ties and suits to work. At home they wore short-sleeved shirts with collars. They paid bills and pushed lawn mowers that had rusting blades. At Easter they produced corsages for their wives and daughters to wear to church. The husbands also drove the cars. They poured the early-evening whiskey and ice and waters and brought the dripping glasses to their wives, who were out sitting on gliders or wicker chairs on the porches.

The husbands and fathers did not swear, or if they did they changed swearwords around—the worst I heard were phrases like "what in the Sam Hill," "cripes," and "that so-and-so." Other expressions of discomfort or anger or dismay, in my family, at least, were "crumb!," "that gripes me," and "curses."

My own father's heritage was Czech and a little German, and my mother's was English, German, and French. I didn't know exactly how to view this: it was for me both special and uncomfortable because almost all of my Saint Paul friends had Irish backgrounds—Faricy, Kelly, Mulrooney, Collins, Conway, O'Connell. I hated going to school on Saint Patrick's Day because I could not legitimately wear green.

Didn't not being Irish mean that my family's Roman Catholicism was a little off center? Our family was such a hodgepodge. My father used to say that he thought we might be part Jewish due to his Eastern European roots and also that, perhaps, there was a little Japanese in the family (some ancestor's last name was Shimoda). I had read somewhere in a book about the "new immigrants" that Catholic Czechs in Minnesota, especially men, took a somewhat wry and rebellious stance toward the Church.

The children of the fathers and mothers were "the boys and the girls." When the children became teenagers they were still referred to as the boys and the girls.

The boys wore white bucks and khaki pants and collared shirts and their hair short, and they caddied or bagged groceries in the summer and went to Catholic military academies during the year. They played hockey or went to Lutsen for skiing in the winter and were altar boys. They drove new Chevrolets if their families had money. They did the Lindy on the dance floors at mixers. Once in a great while they smuggled a Hamm's beer or two out of their parents' houses and then talked about it in whispers for weeks and weeks. Many of the boys smoked.

The girls also smoked: mostly Kents and Salems and Winstons, although sometimes someone brought a few of her mother's English Ovals to slumber parties or some Benson and Hedges or colored cigarettes, which were pretty, with gold around the filter tops, but didn't taste all that good. The girls didn't drink. The closest they had come to a drug was in seventh grade, when they heard that putting two aspirins in a Coke could make a person feel funny (funny peculiar), and they had tried that but soon grew bored with it.

The girls went to Catholic girls' schools and wore nylon stockings with white anklets layered over them, and blue oxford shoes. They wore uniform skirts and jackets and blazers with the school letters embroidered on them in contrasting colors. Uniforms, however, were never to be worn to anything that would even slightly embarrass the school, and when two girls from Our Lady of Peace went to see Elvis Presley in downtown Saint Paul in their uniforms, it was a terrible scandal: they were called in to the principal's office and nearly expelled.

The girls mostly didn't work in the summer; they vied for the attention of the popular boys and if they were successful went swimming with them at Turtle Lake or Lake Phelan or Lake Nokomis. The girls lay out in the sun and some of them who could afford it drove cars. They had slumber parties, at which they didn't sleep, so that the fathers had to come downstairs to where they had their sleeping bags and pillows and say cheerfully, "Ixnay with the atterchay," or, "Pipe down." The slumber parties sometimes included an activity called "slamming," in which the girls thought up things to say that were, from their point of view, bad about certain people.

They went to proms, where, by order of the nuns, they had to wear straps on the formals that were at least two inches wide. Girls who had their ears pierced were considered cheap.

Some girls in my group of friends started going out in freshman year of high school. Always our dates were limited to boys from Cretin (named after Bishop Cretin) or Saint Thomas, which were both Catholic military academies in Saint Paul. Saint

Thomas sponsored chaperoned freshmen mixers about once a month.

I met a boy I liked and at age fourteen I started dating him. After a year or so, we ended up going steady. Until he got his license, his father patiently did the drop-offs and pickups from football games, movies, and from parties, where we danced to 78 rpm records in the knotty-pine-paneled basements of friends' houses.

Toward the end of high school, the boy broke up with me. Afterward, whenever he encountered me, his behavior was—to be generous about it—ambiguous and callow.

When I went to college, though, I met new boys, from Loras, the Catholic men's college in Dubuque, and dated one of them in the spring of 1960. He had just returned to college after serving in the army; he was a sweet young man who was very good to me.

In the convent, of course, the complications of dating would just drop off. The young men of the past would have to eat their hearts out or take to drinking and talking among themselves.

"*God,* can you believe it, she became a nun."

"Don't say 'God.' "

Or, "Oh, no, she doesn't love *me*—she's in love with the *Lord,* for Christ's sake."

"James, have you been drinking?"

Or, "The woman for me is in some convent somewhere."

Or, "Those Catholic girls, especially the ones who join convents, those are the really hot ones."

In the end the boy would get over it and either join the seminary or marry someone who wore her hair in a French twist and who could cook veal scaloppine for company, someone who didn't think much about the language of New York and its brownstones.

I had thought of becoming a nurse, like my sister, and figuring out after that whether I might want to get married and have children, as she had eventually done. I even became a nurse's aide one summer to earn money for expenses at my upcoming first year at college. After that summer, I knew I would not become a nurse.

All those bodies to be bathed, all those back rubs to be given, all those bedpans and urinals to be emptied and rinsed after measuring, keeping track of intake and output of urine and bowels. Eighteen years old and having seen practically nothing of nakedness, I was shocked. The fact that I worked at a Catholic hospital, Saint Joseph's, the hospital where I had been born, did nothing to alleviate this.

All those bodies and body parts and diseases, and at such close range. All the bloody sheets from miscarriages; all the multiple myelomas, hernia repairs, colon cancers; and once, meningitis; and once, radium in someone's vagina. All the catheters and rubber tubes in rectums, which led to what looked like large covered Dixie cups (something to do with gas, I surmised, but I never asked).

I was proud of knowing medical terminology; it was the reality that was overwhelming. There was an empty bed one morning where the cranky Mrs. Brown—her chart read "Terminal CA"—had been for weeks. One man with a colostomy got into a rage and threw his dirty dressings at a nurse. At the beginning of one of my shifts, a man with a tracheotomy begged me for something—what? I couldn't understand a word he said and there was that awful gurgling that accompanied his trying to talk.

Night shift was nice—no bed baths and most people sleeping. On their breaks some of the nurses and nurse's aides went down to the screened-in porch at the end of their wing and smoked. When I smoked I felt better, and all that ailing flesh down the dimly lit hall seemed to recede.

If these things happened to people, what would became of *you* in the end? How could you stand it unless heaven lay beyond? And if you were a nun, surely you would go to heaven. A bride of

Christ? How could He refuse you? And better a teaching nun than a nurse or a nursing nun.

We loved most of our high school nuns, the BVMs, who seemed a different species from our grade school nuns, who happened to be from a different order. The BVMs were individuals, but they had something in common: they were supersmart, whether we had them for solid geometry or biology or Latin or creative writing or drama or American literature. The nuns were immaculate, they were poised, they were organized, they were often funny ("Ken and Don and the boys" was how one Sister referred to the characters when she was teaching *The Marble Faun*). They were understanding, they were hard workers, they were up on modern girls.

We allowed them to know us well. We stayed after school to talk to them about boys, family problems—anything. They were genuinely interested; they were savvy. They made us wonder sometimes if we might have vocations to the religious life.

If you had a vocation, it meant that God was calling you to become a nun. If you screwed up your courage to speak of this to your favorite nun-teacher, and if she was encouraging, if she said she would pray for you, things suddenly changed.

Sister had not treated you as if you were out of your tree; she had not said, "*You?* You're kidding, of course, you who spend half your time considering whether your formal for the Military Ball should be green chiffon or pink net or blue taffeta." The way she spoke to you about this meant that she thought so much of you that she could imagine you as a BVM.

And if the nuns imagined you as one of them, then you started imagining yourself as one of them, even though you could not get past a certain part in your imagining—what went on behind closed doors in the convent. But wasn't this part of the attraction?

What lay behind the sealed door?

. . .

I knew my "Bluebeard." Like my father, who read—looking as if he was having a session with Dr. Mesmer—the *National Geographic* and who read *The Blue Nile* and *The White Nile* over and over again; or like a little cat, I wanted to know certain things: I wanted into the rooms beyond.

I studied the general and special "ends" of the BVM Congregation. The general end of the group was the glory of God and the nuns' own perfection by means of the three simple vows of poverty, chastity, and obedience. The special end of the community was the salvation of their neighbor, to be accomplished by Christian instruction and education imparted by the Sisters in schools. In their Constitutions, each Sister was exhorted to "imbue her pupils with the principles of the true faith." She was supposed to train her students to love God "by the most diligent practice of all virtues; thus, while sowing in their minds the seeds of knowledge, she may unite their souls to God by fervent love."

At the time, all I had a firm grasp on was that the nuns had given themselves completely to God and that they were terrific teachers. This looked good all the way around. It would mean teaching, which I thought I would like; it would mean being really engaged in the intellectual life, which I knew I would like. To do these things and to help my neighbor in a rather direct way to salvation would be a good thing. I mostly thought of my neighbor as the high school girls I would someday teach. They would stay after school and talk to me just as I had once done with the nuns. It would be like prolonging myself, projecting myself into a future environment that would be pleasant.

I was choosing the most perfect state possible in everyone's—Catholics'—estimation. I would be part of an elite, the crème de la crème. The religious life seemed glamorous and restrained. Trying to be the Mistress of Restraint was just my meat. And the BVMs were the only real women intellectuals I knew. Also, all that messy bodily stuff would seem less important, I thought.

Were married people elite? No. I wanted to be thought of as exotic and mysterious, some kind of a heroine. The Maryknoll Sisters were attractive in this way, but I thought they were mostly nurses in jungles, and that would mean contact with body parts again. I could be a surgical nurse like Sister Luke, I supposed; it would help if I dealt with my patients while they were anesthetized rather than when they were squirming or complaining or looking at me with fear and pain in their eyes.

I wanted to be shed of the messy complications of social and family life. I loved God. I wanted to do good. I wanted peace and order, neatness and beauty—and sanctity.

As a nun I wouldn't be wasting time wondering what God's will was for me. My religious superiors would be watchful, not like my father, who often fell asleep in his armchair in the evenings. Superiors would not fall asleep—the thought was ludicrous!—like that. They would be busy looking after my welfare.

To be sure, your religion teachers had said that the world was good because God had created it. But they more often dwelt on the shadow side, where things were muddy and murky, where occasions of sin lurked, where you could slip to your doom.

Why not just give your life, your heart to God, and escape iniquity in all its forms? Why not swat the leafhopper that is always struggling over some horizon like the sun coming up in the east?

There would be clear-cut rules by which you should live. You were a cradle Catholic and now you would be at the apex of Catholic life. You were lucky. You would continue until death with this silver spoon in your mouth.

Black Becomes Us

At five in the morning of my second day in the convent, the rising bell sounded. It was neither carillon nor handbell: it was an electric, awful, rasping clang that seemed to wear itself out rather than to actually end. What were they doing with such a bell in a convent? Were they giving in to the modern world? Bowing to efficiency? It sounded like the bell in my high school, the one that rang as a signal for a change of classes.

I washed and brushed my teeth and then went down to the bathroom with my basin. No one spoke a word.

Back in my alcove, I dressed; I put everything on correctly. I combed my hair and looked at myself in the small chrome-bound space of the mirror. I saw the white band of my collar and the top of my black cape. It looked good.

I made my bed and folded my white pajamas and tucked them under my pillow; I put the makeup mirror into a drawer. Then I pulled back my curtains, pleated them, and tied them to the vertical steel pole.

I saw, as I walked to the chapel, that my fellow postulants looked good, too. Black became us almost thrillingly, I thought. Clerical, but classy. The black and the white. And so easy, just like grade school and high school, where there had been no choices to have to make in the mornings on weekdays.

Never again would there be distinctions among us: nothing that showed who could afford Lanz dresses and Capezio shoes from Frank Murphy's in downtown Saint Paul and who could not, who had good taste and who did not. No more having to analyze, reading *Seventeen* or *Mademoiselle,* what color clothing went with our skin. Were we olive complected, or not?

Did our skin have ivory tones? Forget all that now. We had our blacks.

Mass

When Mass began that morning, we knew we were in the right place. *"Introibo ad altare Dei,"* the priest-celebrant proclaimed after making the sign of the cross: "I will go in unto the altar of God."

"In unto," I always thought, made the whole sentence seem dignified and lovely.

"Ad Deum, qui laetificat juventutem meam": "To God, who giveth joy to my youth."

At an early age in Catholic school I had been taught to think of the Mass in terms of the first letter in the word. Sister had, but only in stages, drawn an *M* on the blackboard.

The first part of the letter could be thought of as a stroke of the chalk or the fountain pen upward: an approach to God. We present ourselves before the altar, are penitent, and reach up to Him: *"Introibo ad altare Dei."*

The next stroke, a downstroke, represents God reaching back toward us in the lessons from scripture, namely, the Epistle and the Gospel.

The second upstroke represents our offering of bread and wine, and so our lives, to God.

He accepts, and after the consecration of these elements gives back to us in the final downstroke (we sighed in appreciation as Sister completed, at last, the whole of the *M*) our offerings transformed into Christ's Body and Blood.

The *M* of the Mass was bold, high drama: a miniseries of brilliant measures. It had mountaintops and swales. It had at least four acts. It had resolution.

Add to this the fluttering missal ribbons, and the liturgical colors proper to the Church Year, and the reverberations of the organ, and the pure beeswax candles, and your family there (all dressed up, sober, dignified), and the receiving of the stiff Chi-Rho-embossed host onto your tongue, the feel of it melting (since you did not chew it), its cardboardy taste. It became participative opera, more stirring than *Carmen,* darker than *Don Giovanni.*

This dramaturgy bore the weight of the past and the promise of a future. And it was performed impeccably, as far as you knew, every single day all over the world. Heaven and earth might fade away, but the Mass would never fade away.

The Sermon

The sermon at that first Mass in the convent was addressed directly to us, the new postulants. The priest said that God had implanted the desire to be a Sister of Charity of the Blessed Virgin Mary in each one of us.

You *had* that desire.

Not only that, he said, but we had actually been accepted by the community, and since God had inspired that acceptance, it must be a sign that we had a vocation. He said that we should therefore cast aside all doubt, that we should not reconsider our generous decision to give ourselves completely to the religious life and to Christ.

. . .

Well, *you* weren't going to reconsider. Father's conclusion struck you as not just logical, but as a kind of sacred logic.

Any signs, he said, that arose to suggest we should not be there would be given to our superiors, and they would make this known to us. But in general, he didn't want us to waste time thinking about it.

You *wouldn't* waste time that way.

We were also not to worry if we felt ourselves missing those we had left behind. Those affections were good and wholesome, he said. He said that now those affections could be transferred to God, Who is the greatest good of all; in fact, every other good is swallowed up in Him.

You questioned Father's generalization about "wholesome" as you remembered the demurring you did over the attempt at unbuttoning a blouse button in the backseat of a car. Probably Father was a little naive.

But *all right*. You would be like the Jonah of old. God could swallow you up. And you would be like Mary Poppins minus her bag: all the goods packed away in your huge valise could be swallowed up by Him, too.

Routines

We fell right into a daily routine from almost that second day forward. Mass, following communal prayer, began at 6 a.m.

After Mass, while the kitchen novices were preparing to serve breakfast, we were led outside to walk down the Pine Walk, which extended about the length of a city block and ended in the convent cemetery.

Then breakfast came, and then a domestic duty. Instructions in the postulate were followed by noontime "Examen" in the chapel.

Mentions of Examen occur early in that classic retreat guide, *The Spiritual Exercises of Saint Ignatius,* though the word itself comes from the Latin *examen* (a means of weighing or measuring; the tongue or needle of a balance). At midday we knelt to privately review and reflect on the morning that had just passed; we examined our consciences. Had we committed any sins? What faults or defects had we seen in ourselves? This amounted to an hour-by-hour scrutiny of thoughts, words, and deeds. Having taken this measure, we expressed our prayerful sorrow, asked forgiveness of the Lord, and resolved to do better.

The whole exercise of self-scrutiny, this noontime intensification of what I did a little too much of anyway, left me depressed. Scrupulosity could be a vice and was not recommended by anyone, but it tended to grow like mold in the culture of all this measuring.

Immediately after Examen we had dinner in the refectory, followed by more Instructions, followed by a short period of recreation, when we could speak with one another. Spiritual reading time was in the afternoon, and then prayer in the chapel before a light supper.

In the evening there was another recreation period, followed by prayer. And then to bed.

We did seem to fall into this daily routine as into a pool of water. Or we had already fallen the day we decided we had vocations. Or we were led, carried into the pool.

The thing that many of us did not do was dive. Babies, surprisingly, can be taught to take to swimming. The thing babies cannot be taught to do is to dive.

The rule book, or Constitutions, spelled out the work routines.

MEANS FOR PRESERVING DISCIPLINE: WORK

115. No one may undertake any work which seems to be beyond her strength; but if such should be enjoined, let her inform the Superior and be ready to do whatever the Superior, after having examined the matter, shall deem expedient in the Lord.

116. Idleness, as the origin of all evil, they shall diligently shun; and if after they have fulfilled all that belongs to their duty, time be left, it must be employed in other occupations befitting the condition of each Sister. If they have no such occupation, let them apply to the Superior to learn what they are to do.

117. They shall never be allowed to keep in the houses of the Congregation any animal in the feeding and care of which time is often uselessly spent.

I knew there would be domestic work. My imagining convent life included scrub brushes and buckets because I knew the story about my grandmother making a surprise visit to her Dominican-novice daughter and finding her in the convent entryway, scrubbing the floor. Grandmother Peil had thrown a fit to see Cleopha down on her hands and knees.

But whereas I expected scrub brushes and buckets, something on a grand scale, I was assigned to a small vegetable peeler. I worked with several other postulants preparing vegetables and fruits for the kitchen crew for the noon and evening meals. We sat around a large stainless steel table and peeled apples, potatoes, rutabagas. We sliced rhubarb and diced carrots. All this peeling and chopping was done in silence.

Occasionally, a potato peel shot off the peeler and flew up in someone's face or landed on someone's arm or in someone's lap.

Isn't something getting out of control in a holy place funnier than it would be otherwise? The bishop's miter at an angle, the altar boy tripping, a bat loose in church. A loud sneeze, a hiccup.

A potato peel hitting a postulant on the cheek.

A couple of us laughed. Someone frowned: laughter, even though it involved no real articulation of vowels and consonants, would be against the spirit of the silence we were supposed to be keeping.

I thought it was funny. But I more or less contained myself.

Silence

During August, in daily lessons called Instructions, we had begun to learn about silence. There was a rule of silence, part of the monastic tradition, and we would follow it.

But none of this would be imposed on us. We freely chose religious life. We freely chose to follow our callings, or vocations.

If . . . then. If we had so done—if we had chosen to be nuns— *then* we had chosen silence as part of the Holy Rule of our community. We could always leave.

But, you thought, not if you have a vocation; if you have a vocation you don't leave. You certainly wouldn't walk out the door on a vocation. This was the choice of all choices. Therefore accepting the discipline of silence followed as night followed day or as following the Marlboro Man meant following someone who was rugged.

.　.　.

On the surface, silence was simple: we didn't speak unless it was necessary.

But what was the point of silence? The point was, we learned, not mere silence, not silence to preserve some sort of order, but something much greater. In silence the idea was to recollect ourselves, to place ourselves more squarely in the presence of God than we would if people were talking to us all the time. We could pray, we could meditate, we could contemplate.

This habit, this way of living, was not altogether foreign to me. My sister, Judy, was eight years older; my brother, Damon, was six and a half years older. I could not keep pace with their changing interests and activities, and although I had friends, I was often alone and amused myself. I read; I played paper dolls; I played with my tin dollhouse; I played dress-up; I made leaf houses. I had sewing cards and finger paint. I had plaster of Paris kits with little rubber molds.

I looked carefully, in the silence, at the shrubs and at tree bark in the large yard of the corner house in which we lived. Opening up the insides of bridal wreath and lilac stems by biting them, I then chewed them. I walked out by myself in a bathing suit in the Minnesota summer rains. I lay down in the grass and stared at the undersides of tulips as they grew.

Silence worked for me, or rather, it worked *on* me in many ways. In the convent, where we were all short on real privacy, silence gave us some space. It seemed, most of the time, benevolent.

And sometimes the silence was downright full, as in the Gerard Manley Hopkins poem where "Elected Silence" beats upon the "whorlèd ear" and becomes, in its stillness, musical.

I never heard any mystical being speak in the silences, nor had I literally heard heavenly music as some of the saints had done. The sound of rushing air in the chapel came not from a gigantic Holy Spirit but from those horizontal windmills, the huge ceiling fans.

Silence was broken, of course, by people doing things they could not control—coughing, sneezing—by short periods of recreation, and by the sounds of work being done. Brillo pads scratched on the oversized cooking pots and pans after the noon dinner. It seemed that an electric buffer was always buzzing, pressing tight against the waxed floors. Someone might drop a hymnal. But all of this merely emphasized the silence rather than disturbing it.

Sounds could never absorb this silence; nothing could order it around. It concentrated itself, and from it all else flowed. Silence could never be silenced.

What was it? It was a thing.

There was also the Solemn, or Grand, Silence (the phrases, with their capital letters, seemed elegant, aristocratic), which began later in the evening, around nine, when the electric bell would go off to warn us. Then we *really* didn't speak unless it was necessary. It ended after Mass in the morning, after our encounter with Christ in the Eucharist—Holy Communion.

The practical distinction between the two silences was not quite clear to me, but it went something like this: during the regular hours of silence, if a Sister didn't see something or know something that she really needed to know, you could speak a word to her about this. During the Grand Silence, you would—or I would—hesitate to do this. However, if she, say, slipped on something and hurt herself, you could call for aid for her. So it wasn't totally ridiculous.

Occasionally, during the Grand Silence, a basin would slip from a pair of hands. Clang. Another clang.

Clang clang.

Then it was bouncing.

When we heard this, we knew. A basin had gone down.

The sound of it must have reached almost every recess in the convent: somewhere all the mice must have paused; the bats in the attic must have unfolded their wings and started off the rafters.

When the noncompliant, unholy basin, that Helmet of Mambrino, went rolling down the staircase, and water—sometimes clean, sometimes soapy and dirty—splashed everywhere, splashed onto the dark wood of steps or banister during the Grand Silence, we were silent but not always paralyzed. We could play Sancho; we could help retrieve the basin for the averted eyes and flushed or pale face of its owner, and we could help wipe up the puddles.

Occasionally the basin dropper was trying not to laugh, and this was a more complex situation: she would feel guilty about her laughter rising to the surface. If *we* laughed when we saw *her* trying not to laugh, later she would feel even guiltier.

This laughing issue again. First at vegetable duty and now here. I tried to be above all of that. Some of these girls, I self-righteously said to myself as I watched them laughing, are really quite immature.

Marbles

From the sitting pulpit came instruction in how to carry ourselves: correct posture. The BVMs in high school had taught us a unit on social graces, but in the convent we were in a realm of even more detail, not to speak of admonishment.

We should think of our bodies as being made up of three marbles: one was the head, one was the trunk, one was the legs. Printed diagrams accompanied the marbles metaphor.

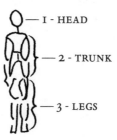

— 1 - HEAD

— 2 - TRUNK

— 3 - LEGS

Nothing was left to the imagination, as in the genuflection marbles:

GENUFLECT.
Two top marbles
directly in line.
Keep the right knee
opposite the left
ankle.

Or the kneeling marbles:

KNEEL.
Keep two top marbles
in line; equal pressure
on both knees.

In walking, the marbles were to be in line, of course, with a relaxed movement of the arms. Our thumbs were to be to the back. We were not to swing past our black skirts with our arms; we were to place our weight on the entire foot and move from the hips. We were supposed to FLOAT, in capital letters.

I loved this. I loved details and metaphors. And I loved putting things into practice.

The handout sheets proceeded to tell us what we should not

do, again in terms of the marble stick figures. We should not be the Automatic Washer, agitating our hips. Neither should we be the Breaststroke Walker:

BREASTSTROKE WALKER.
Swings shoulders and arms as in swimming.

The Dip and Diver showed a swayback with the stomach leading and too much bending of the knees. The Bunny Hop Walker—we smiled at one another when we saw this—went walking and bouncing on the balls of her feet.

Miss Mincer Steps took steps too small for the size of her body, and Barrel Shoulders walked with round shoulders and a bent head. Throwing the entire body forward and taking steps that were too large placed a young woman in the category of the Lunger, whereas the Leaning Tower favored one shoulder in the way she walked.

Swivel Shoulder's problem was immediately apparent to us. Finally, the Skater walked much too quickly and dragged her feet: naturally, her marbles were way out of alignment.

We practiced and practiced.

Did anyone think, *When is this class going to be over?* Or did anyone think, in spite of herself or not, *Isn't it time to go home now?*

Other Graces

More handouts, more dispatches came from the immaculate, manicured, rosy-faced Sister C. in her proper position in the sitting pulpit.

The well-groomed postulant, for instance, bathed or showered every day (but did not take too long at it). She used a deodorant and washed her hair frequently. Washing her hands often was important—she should be especially careful to remove ink and vegetable stains promptly. She cleaned her nails daily, filed them weekly, pushed back the cuticle when drying her hands. Teeth were to be brushed at least twice a day, and stockings and lingerie—this was beginning to sound like *Seventeen* magazine—changed every day. A clean handkerchief was always to be carried in the pocket and shoes were to be polished regularly.

Do nothing in public, one handout said, that calls attention to the functions of the body. Stifle a yawn; cover the mouth. When coughing or sneezing is necessary, try to do it inconspicuously and quietly.

Avoid throat clearing, scratching, cleaning out the ears, picking the face or teeth, spitting, and similar unpleasant acts in public. All those gross acts named in one patch of prose on a convent handout struck me as funny. The handout may as well have read, "This is not the zoo, girls."

There was more:

Knees are never crossed.

No lolling or sprawling.

We should never walk with a heavy tread.

It is unbecoming in a Religious to think of herself
first, taking the best in working equipment, food, or
place.

Don't hold your finger on the elevator button.

Avoid gesticulating unnecessarily when speaking.

Never stretch in public.

When speaking to anyone, particularly to one of our
Superiors, we should not gaze around, but look at her.

Disregard others' mistakes. Accept apologies.

All letters should be folded correctly and good form
should be used.

We should be most careful that what we say is not
offensive to others. Critical remarks should not be
made.

We should not interrupt others when they are speaking.

Welcome one returned.

Answer questions. Refrain from asking unnecessary
questions.

We should not lean against the door, walls, or furniture;
nor should we slouch.

Do the most unpleasant task yourself.

We should never stand or sit in an unrestrained manner.

A loud and aggressive tone of voice is unbecoming; also
loud laughter.

Slang is entirely out of place and not permitted.

We should not call to another across a considerable
distance.

Never brush by another without begging pardon. Go
behind when possible.

Hand things to another with the right hand, palm up.

Left hand when passing to the left.

We were to remember that the "cultivated woman NEVER seems to be in a hurry." In conversation one personal anecdote does not call for another (don't play "Can you top this?"). *Don't* think, we were instructed, that "you have to say something brilliant all the time." In conversation, don't "let the talk die in your hand." Don't ask personal questions, don't discuss your own health, don't speak in a studied and artificial way.

Start where your hearer's mind is and give undivided attention. Use tact, which is really spiritual diplomacy: say, "How well you look," instead of, "How much better you look." "Make it easy for listeners to follow the train of thought."

There were more instructions, one of which was that the "secret of being tiresome is to tell everything."

Us Again

Early on we were taught how we should think about friendships between us. We were not to engage in what was called a "particular friendship"; this meant that we were not to develop a close, special relationship with anyone. A section in our rule book explained how doing so would be against mutual charity.

As my mother, standing stock-still and wide-eyed—quoting Sylvester the cat in the Tweety Bird cartoons—would say, "*That* sounds *logical!*" It sounded logical to me. *If . . . then.* If you have special friends, then someone may feel left out.

None of us, I thought, will ever feel left out again. Not one of you, I thought, looking at my set sitting up straight in their chairs in the postulate, will have to worry about being a zero.

If you were a little boring, you would still feel worthy of care. If you were homely or clumsy, basic caring would still come your way. If you were seen as prissy or as a bit sloppy, care remained. If you were seen as failing, you would be admonished, yes, but care would not be withdrawn from you.

You will always feel worthy of being talked to; no one, walking into a room, will dodge you in favor of someone else. All your fears of being abandoned, of being left standing in line when they were down to choosing left field for the softball team, will be somewhat assuaged.

Practically speaking, this meant that I did not spend too much time with anyone, that we did not pair off during recreation periods and have long heart-to-heart discussions. The sharing of private jokes or private struggles would have been frowned upon as too particular. Seeking certain people out again and again at recreation would be particular.

I started immediately, of course, to follow the rule.

All the little bright threads of connections between me and others started to fade. Stop talking so much to the witty and expressive Lucy, an already accomplished stage director, I said to myself. Forget about finding out about what lies behind Jane's winsome smile.

But what should I do about my friends from Saint Paul—with Tessa and Kathy? Our friendship had already paled because of the silence we were observing. Now I would have to distance myself even more. They had been particular friends and now there was a rule against that. So let them go.

I withdrew. Though I was pleasant enough to others, I began to concentrate so hard on being a good postulant that the other young women in my set looked small and far away, as if I were seeing them through the wrong end of a pair of field glasses.

To stay generally within the confines of the rule and still in some sense reach out to them as persons was beyond me. My style was one of restraint, perfectionistic and reserved. I'd keep my spine straight.

Just *watch* how I can keep this rule. *I'll* keep this rule. My sails will be trimmed precisely. I was in no mood for particular friendships. Didn't that mean I was getting holier?

And getting holier was what I wanted to do. If I felt uncertain about myself, about my withdrawing, never mind. Now *something* certain lay at my very center: the Good. The Good, the Perfect. The Holy. Jesus.

I couldn't have friends. But I did start watching people closely. Noting physical details became an alternate way to know or at least to guess at the inner lives of others. I read faces, eyebrows, foreheads, twitches, gestures; a hand turned up to expose a palm, a dogged walk, a quizzical expression, a faltering answer to a Superior.

That one doesn't like rhubarb, I thought. This one is embarrassed at being caught out not paying attention at Instructions. What does it cost that other one to look so cheerful all of the time?

Sneezy, Dopey, Sleepy

Few things disrupted the silence that grew and grew during the postulancy. But some uneasiness formed; some vague agitation surfaced. Not smoking.

Not smoking began to dog me. This is what it is like to quit smoking, I thought. A lot of the time, all I wanted was a cigarette.

In my worst moments, and with some shame, I thought of

bailing out—for cigarettes. It was hard to imagine going on and on with no Kents after breakfast. While taking notes in my notebook, would there be no Winstons ever again? In the late afternoon, no Salems? Or when I was out of cigarettes, no English Ovals to borrow from my mother?

Where *was* my mother, anyway?

An amputee you were, without cigarettes. You had multiple phantom limbs like multiple personalities, and all of you ached all day.

One thing helped ease my withdrawal. I was taking a drug.

It was August now and I was sneezing with the hay fever that used to cause my family to stay indoors, to take turns lying on the living room couch, to prompt my mother to wash our handkerchiefs and then boil them in a kettle on the stove. My eyes brimmed and spilled over, reacting to allergens: some mornings when I woke, I couldn't see for my eyelids being pasted shut.

This drug, the one I was allowed to bring with me into the convent, was called Pyribenzamine, something quite commonly prescribed in those days. It stopped my sneezing and itching and weeping so I could go about, even in a dazed way, the life of the mind and spirit.

It made me so sleepy that I felt like a drunk, though I didn't know why it should do this to me. And I didn't care to learn why.

Drugs and their effects were science in the early 1960s, and you didn't think you could possibly be a scientific type, even if your high school biology teacher *had* asked you if you had considered biology as a career.

Besides, was there really an inside to your body? You didn't think about it.

. . .

I sat before the prow of that ship in the postulate like a sailor on grog. My superiors didn't seem to notice.

However, the sedation seemed to help a little with the not smoking. It kept my withdrawal somewhat at bay at times.

It kept other withdrawals at bay as well. Did I miss anything in those days? Did I miss my mother, my father, my brother, my sister, my bedroom with its walls painted antique gold, my old boyfriend, my books?

I *guess,* I said to myself.

Under sedation, do you need a family as much? It's easier not to look into your needs.

Under sedation, you can avoid those depths where you would get water in your nose, sputter, flinch, spot the surface, and break it up in the process of finding your way back to the bright air.

Let the things of the deep stay away, way out beyond the drop-offs, way beyond the black lips of the surf. You do not want to push off from Woods Hole or Nantucket or Ilwaco. You do not want to go out across a bar like the Columbia River's to be at the mercy of the sea.

You do not want to go down *in* there, to that sighing world, to those fishy chambers. Let the scientists, let those irreligious and jaunty marine biologists of the flesh, go down there, not you.

Custody of the Eyes

I was sleepy into August and September but not too sleepy to pay attention to Instructions, delivered by Sister C. Instructions came right after chores. One day we began to discuss custody of the eyes.

In the religious practice of custody of the eyes, we were to lower our eyes slightly during periods of silence when, say, walking down a hall or taking a brief walk outside after Mass. The line of vision would angle toward floor or pavement or ground.

We cast our gazes down just enough so that we could see where we were going and see where obstacles lay but also enough so that we would not take in everything that lay in the environment and so that we would not make eye contact with persons. If we saw every flapping window shade, turned to look into every room, took in every expression on the faces of women we met in the hall, we would be distracted. We would be less able to concentrate on the presence of God.

I found this reasonable and quite easy to do.

There was not much new day by day to see inside the convent itself anyway. But if it had not been for custody of the eyes while traveling the Pine Walk out to the community cemetery, I might have seen chipping sparrows, horned larks, chickadees, and nuthatches.

Instead, I concentrated on limiting my vision: holding my head erect, I fixed my eyes so that my line of sight went down at a forty-five-degree angle to the floor, turned toward my feet at another forty-five-degree angle, and turned again at a right angle to my body, traveling more or less straight back up to my eyes.

And this custody, it was just like Gabrielle, Sister Luke, from my teenage reading. I think I could hardly wait to lower the flashlight of my eyes. A curtain, an invisible veil, had rung partway down over my sight.

In the fifties I had hats with veils, and when I put one on and looked at myself in the mirror, something powerful under that black or white netting had happened. I had become more exotic.

The downcast eyes, the lowered gaze: at the beginning, custody of the eyes seemed so pure, beautiful, mysterious. Besides allowing oneself to concentrate on God, it suggested the hidden, the hidden depths, something hooded.

The difficulty was—there was no one there to appreciate it. Sister Luke's young man, Jean, her former romantic interest, showed up at her investiture as a novice. My taking the veil was decidedly not a public ceremony. None of my old boyfriends would have dared to appear. And the bishop and his assistants surely didn't dwell on me. They probably had to be in Cedar Rapids by noon for another ceremony.

Who would see how mysterious and contained I looked? Who would see the way I walked, practicing custody of the eyes with almost perfect form? Who would convince me that I was still there?

God saw me, to be sure. But He knew everything: nothing about my past, present, or future need be discovered by Him. He knew it all.

There were no dwarfs to hold their candles above me and say, "Oh, lovely, oh, lovely," to say that I was just a plain lovely child as all children are lovely. Even if there had been dwarfs I probably wouldn't have spotted them.

Who, exactly, *was* passing me in the hall? With custody of the eyes, no wonder murderers, desecrators, intrusives, and predators of all sorts had it so easy once they got into some convents, seminaries, and abbeys. Especially if they had thought to look like nuns or monks from the knees down, close to the floor.

Now both silence and custody of the eyes characterized my life. One by one the practices, the rules, the disciplines accumulated and attached themselves to me. Or I attached myself to them. By the grace of God.

Prayer

We had regular communal prayer. We said morning prayers, the rosary, evening prayers, and on weekends something called the Little Office (as opposed to the full Holy Office, which included Matins, Lauds, Prime, Terce, Sext, None, Vespers, and Compline).

We also had a great deal of instruction in individual prayer and meditation, what could be called contemplative prayer, which I thought fit my temperament. It was a more focused species, but a species nevertheless of what I had known in so many hours of solitary play in my youth. The silences again, but informed by the exercise of my imagination.

I had numerous sets of paper dolls and plastic dollhouse dolls, the ones that bent at the waist and the knees, the ones whose arms could swing freely. My dolls did things and went places, changed clothes a lot, but they mostly stayed home and had conversations. They talked to one another; they talked to themselves. I believe that they were thoughtful. My dolls led vivid lives.

I also came to the convent having often meditated on the mysteries of my faith and especially on the mysteries associated with the decades of the rosary: the Joyful, the Sorrowful, the Glorious Mysteries. While I was saying ten Hail Marys out loud or privately, for example, I would try to visualize the Annunciation: I saw Mary at prayer, saw the angel appearing, saw Mary nodding her head while speaking her *"Fiat."*

Our instructions in prayer were lengthy and frequent and complicated but generally accessible. The mimeographed handouts on prayer were interesting; one, by Romano Guardini, a popular European theologian, carefully qualified and refined:

there were lots of "however's" and "at the same time's" and "step by step's."

However much you used subject matter in your prayer, visualization was not the end. You wanted somehow to be in conversation with God; you wanted to make some contact. You wanted to let Him know you adored Him, or you told Him how sorry you were for your sins, or you thanked Him for something. It was also appropriate to ask Him for something, always with the condition that His will in the end be done, not yours. The intellect and the feelings and the senses were all mustered.

And the will. For at the end of the meditation and prayer, the idea was that your will would be moved. You saw something you should do to be more virtuous; you determined to be more charitable, less selfish. Or perhaps, more simply, you felt yourself loving God more, admiring Him more.

Sometimes you felt "dry," singularly uninvolved, and that was all right, was normal from time to time. Sometimes you simply rested in His presence.

Though many of us from time to time felt elated during periods of prayer, none of us—that I knew of—went into pronounced ecstasies. If someone had, and then had spoken of this, our superiors would have been somewhat alarmed and would have scrutinized her very, very carefully.

Were you supposed to hear God, though, in some mild way or other? Was He supposed to speak back? You were encouraged to listen to Him. And how could you be sure He was talking? Sometimes He sounded strangely like the Fathers of the Church or even like our superiors.

Something

But sometimes during periods of prayer and meditation, as I knelt or sat or stood or walked, I stopped thinking about aligning my marbles and getting my prayer life "right"; and I did feel awed and comforted. I felt God as categorically different from anyone I knew or had read or had heard speak.

Underneath the silences, behind my maidenly downcast eyes, I felt something. Undeniably, almost unaccountably, something that felt authentic was building: a sense of Presence. I'm sure that others in my set felt it, too. We didn't speak of this.

The heels of our black shoes were soft. We were to keep to one side of the hall, close to the wall; we were never to walk right down the center of any passageway. We made no noise; we went catlike from place to place like Carl Sandburg's spooky fog, and sometimes, I think, we even spooked ourselves.

But we could also live with ourselves, we found out. We didn't have to be talking with someone all the time or listening to music all the time. We didn't have to be doing anything all the time or any of the time. We learned what containment felt like. And at the center of it for me was Something, not nothing.

On the other hand, like the acquiring of any habits or the ridding yourself of them for a higher purpose or cause, there were drawbacks. In those self-conscious first days, first weeks, first months, you watched yourself like a hawk. You were full of yourself. You got worn out. Sometimes you'd think it was heartburn. Hopkins, the poet-priest, had gotten spiritual heartburn, too. He summed up the unpleasantness: "my taste was me."

Wieners

Smoking's fingers began to loosen a little around my neck. Mostly, at this point, I didn't think about it. Bad days occurred when the professed Sisters had visitors in the front parlors. That smell of cigarettes renewed my struggle.

Something else happened, to my chagrin. I seemed to be looking forward to eating. All the time. I had heard that smoking suppressed appetite; now I believed it. In place of smoke, I wanted to inhale my food.

In the very beginning, in the refectory, I had not been very hungry and had focused not on the food but on the spiritual reading, which occurred mostly at lunch, or what in the convent was called dinner. From yet another sitting pulpit equipped with a microphone a professed Sister would read a meditation or something from the life of a saint or from a not-too-abstract book of theology.

But now I was a little distracted from the spiritual reading by the food at the table. "Eat to live," we were taught in our morning instructions, and, "Do not live to eat."

This was a hard saying. There was Sunday breakfast, for instance, which consisted of coffee or milk in our coffee cups, sweet rolls from the convent Bake House, and wieners. These last, without buns, were never referred to, in the convent, as what we had called them at home—hot dogs.

At our first Sunday breakfast, we gazed in silence at the off-white platters of unadorned hot dogs and tried not to look at one another. Hot dogs for breakfast? Perhaps they were inexpensive and also easy to serve, where so many people were involved.

I ate few hot dogs by choice before I joined the convent, but now I looked forward to them because they were there and I could smell them and I was always hungry.

We soon learned the proper way to eat wieners just as we learned the proper way to eat bananas. ("Only monkeys pull down the peel and commence eating bananas. Do not do this.") Wieners were to be cut into small pieces on our plates. I ate mine as slowly as I could: I tasted the meat, the meaty juice, and the salt. I began to live for wieners.

Perhaps there would be seconds. If the people at my table wanted more of something, the bowls or platters were placed at one corner of the table, at the end where the professed Sister sat; then a server who stood next to one of the wooden pillars in the refectory and who was always on the alert would come to get the dish, go to the kitchen with it, and bring it back with more of the food in question, should there be any left.

I hoped that there would be wieners left. But the question was, how *many* wieners would return on the plate? And the next question was, how many at our table would want a second wiener?

Sometimes, because we were taught to be watchful and generous, some of us who wanted wieners might pass them up. Once in a while when, say, just three wieners came back for the table of ten, someone who really wanted a wiener would make a partial sacrifice, would cut a wiener in half on the platter, and take one half for herself.

All this was accomplished with dignity, in silence.

When you were nineteen, Catholic, and female in 1960, wieners were probably just wieners, one type of meat among many types of meat we ate in those days: calves' liver and bacon, canned corned beef hash, wieners, chicken croquettes. Even much later on in your life when someone made a joke, you were sincerely uncomprehending.

A Grapefruit Incident

One morning, in silence, at breakfast, there was a grapefruit incident.

A professed Sister, Sister G., of some age and stature and with reddish cheeks, had lately come to reside at the motherhouse for a reason that is not clear. She sat at the head of one of the tables at the refectory, at the table to which I had been assigned.

We had all been served grapefruit with our meal and as usual no one's grapefruit half had been cut into sections. This was not remarkable, I thought: how could the kitchen novices possibly cut grapefruits for three hundred people who are sitting down to eat all at once?

Sister G. had a utensil next to her plate that none of the others, the postulants, had: it was a grapefruit cutting knife. She cut her grapefruit, neatly separating the sections from their membranes. She put the knife down, picked up her spoon, and then glanced down the length of her table.

The rest of us sawed, in silence, at our grapefruit with our dull coffee spoons. Here and there grapefruit juice squirted up in the air. The sections were getting mashed; not much grapefruit was actually getting eaten.

Sister G. looked up. She looked up again, from one place setting to the other, from one struggling postulant to the other.

She frowned.

She sighed—or snorted?—with her lips pressed together. She turned to the postulant on her right and remarked, "You mean you postulants have not been given something so you can cut your grapefruit?"

Shocked, we did not know what to do. Since a professed Sister had spoken, breaking the silence, did that mean we should break silence and answer? Perhaps someone should just shake her head, *No*. No knives for the grapefruit.

I felt a little guilty for watching what was going on.

The postulant who had been addressed decided to answer. "No, Sister."

Sister G., the red of her cheeks deepening, gestured toward the young woman's grapefruit and said, "Give it to me."

And then she had everyone at the table pass her grapefruit down to her and she, unhurriedly, cut each one into sections.

We knew what this meant: when the little handbell was rung as a signal to rise from breakfast, we would not be ready. Sister G. would still be cutting grapefruit. What would we do? Everyone was supposed to rise at the same time.

The bell rang.

Sister G. looked down the oilcloth at us, once. Then she returned to her careful, stubborn cutting.

Everyone else filed out of the refectory trying to avoid looking at the table from which nine postulants had not risen.

This behavior on Sister G.'s part seemed audacious to me. What could she have been thinking, looking so clearly disgusted like that? Was her view that the young postulants and novices had as much right to grapefruit knives as the professed Sisters? Was this a criticism of hierarchical functioning?

Were we worth that much, that we should be given grapefruit knives?

But if we had not been given grapefruit knives by someone in authority in our convent, didn't this mean that it was God's will that we should not have grapefruit knives? After all, we would eventually make, along with vows of poverty and chastity, a vow of obedience—what we were told to do, or where we were sent, was, by virtue of the superior's order, our path to holiness.

The Great Chain of Being

We began, in Instructions, to pore over the Constitutions (known in many religious orders as the Holy Rule), which outlined the way life would be regulated in our particular community. The rule book—slim, small, leather-bound, with a silken marker ribbon—was given into our hands and was the only book save a Bible that we might have for personal use. I now had two books to put in my little drawer in the postulate.

The vows of poverty, chastity, and obedience among other things were explicated in the Constitutions. Take obedience, for instance:

> 102. By the vow of Obedience a Sister takes upon herself the obligation of obeying the formal precept of her lawful Superior in those things which pertain directly or indirectly to the life of the Congregation, that is, to the observance of the vows and of the Constitutions.
>
> 103. By the virtue of Obedience a Sister is under the obligation of conforming to the regulations both of the Constitutions and of her Superiors.
>
> 104. By force of the vow a Sister is bound to obey then only when her lawful Superior commands expressly in virtue of Holy Obedience.
>
> 105. Superiors will rarely, cautiously, and prudently command in virtue of Holy Obedience, and only for grave cause. It is expedient, moreover, that a formal precept be imposed in writing or at least in the presence of two witnesses.
>
> 106. Local Superiors of small houses will abstain from

imposing formal precepts, unless for a very urgent reason. They shall immediately inform the Major Superior.

107. Let the Obedience of all the Sisters be such that everywhere and always they subject themselves completely and with great humility to the will of their Superior; so that in all things in which sin does not manifestly appear they render to their Superior, whoever she may be, whether amiable or severe, that Obedience of which our Lord has given so sublime an example, since they should understand that they are obeying not man, but God Himself, in the person of the Superior.

108. To promote more and more the welfare and the end of this Congregation, it is very necessary that all the Sisters render perfect Obedience not only to their legitimate Superior but also to the Sisters who take her place.

109. While traveling, the Sisters will be subject to the one designated by the Superior.

110. At the Superior's voice and at the sound of the bell, let all be most ready to obey instantly, leaving any occupation whatever.

All these rules and the links between them seemed like the chains I used to make when I was little. I pasted together colorful crepe paper strips, making circlets that I interlinked. The longer the fancy chain, the better I liked it: here the Pope and God were holding one end, the superior was lifting it in the middle to keep it from sagging, and I would be holding the other end.

Point 107 under the section on the "Vow and Virtue of Obedience" could not be clearer: the Sisters should submit themselves (unless it would be sinful to do so) "everywhere and always" to the will of their superior. Further, the Sisters should understand that they are obeying "not man, but God Himself, in the person of the Superior."

Who would have any questions after reading that?

Undoubtedly, some of us did. But we didn't ask them.

For I knew the story: the Sister Luke of my book had worried that an older Sister, Sister Pauline, would not pass the tropical medicines course they were taking together, or would at least fall in score way beneath her own. One day Sister Luke, confessing as a fault her natural antipathy toward Sister Pauline, also asked her superior, Mother Marcella, what she might do to help her peer.

After some thought, Mother Marcella said: "Would you, Sister Luke, be big enough, tall enough to fail your examinations to show humility?"

And brilliant Sister Luke, the only daughter of the foremost chest surgeon in Belgium, "swayed on her knees as if the floor had moved."

True, Mother Marcella had put it as a question, not as an order.

Clearly, and I understood this even when I was sixteen or seventeen, an order given by a superior was to be obeyed. But when she asked a leading question like that, was it just a question? What did she want? Was it a matter of obedience, or of humility? Or both? And how to decide?

I had clutched *The Nun's Story* and read. This was even more suspenseful than Nancy Drew and the mystery of the hidden staircase.

I read that Sister Luke prayed about this matter of failing. The day of the examination came. And when the malariologist, one of six doctors on the governing board, asked her the first question, which was to give a résumé of the special clinical types of pernicious malaria, Sister Luke ran through these types in her head: *cerebral, algid, bilious remittent, blackwater, and the broncho-pneumonic form . . .*

She uttered an interior prayer that God's will be done, and then—"she began to speak."

At this point in the novel, Kathryn Hulme had a two-line

paragraph break, a white space, and I saw no more of the examination scene.

Oh!

Kathryn Hulme, why did you stop that scene just there? I thought. *I want to know what happened.*

In a paragraph after the two-line break, I learned that Sister Luke had passed her exams. And I filled in what must, of course, have been her response: "Cerebral, algid, bilious remittent, blackwater, and the bronchopneumonic form . . ."

News

We had no news from the outside world except personal mail. No news didn't seem to bother me. I was in a drowse anyway. When the very most important news came, the end of the world, we would know. Maybe we would be the first to know, to hear the trumpet being blown by the angel.

Our mail was passed out with the envelopes very neatly slit open.

Our superior read our mail before we received it and before we sent our own letters home to our families. We knew this.

Later on, when the first visit from family was allowed at Mount Carmel, my mother asked me a question.

"Did you like the card from Peter Tewkesbury?"

"Peter Tewkesbury?"

At home, my mother and I had watched some daytime TV together: *The Big Payoff* and *The Price Is Right*. One of the shows' producers was Peter Tewkesbury, and Mother loved that name. It sounded so British. "Look at that," she would always say when the credits rolled. "Peter Tewkesbury. What a wonderful name. Distinguished."

So my humorous mother, who often wrote to me in the convent, had decided to send a greeting card signed "Peter Tewkesbury." We agreed that the reason I had never received it was that
my superior had thought it was from an old boyfriend. It hadn't
passed the screening, distinguished name or no.

We had no newspapers, no television, no radio. But we knew
that the 1960 United States presidential election would occur in
November. We knew when we entered the convent that a
Catholic, John F. Kennedy, was running for president.

I had never paid much attention to what was going on in the
United States but this was special. It was also nice that Mr.
Kennedy was handsome and that his wife, Jacqueline, was pretty
and polished.

Would he win? *Please,* I prayed, *let him win.* A Catholic in the
White House.

We did hear bits about the campaign from Sister C. but
we might as well have been in Bora-Bora or on Easter Island for
all the details we got. Sitting in Dubuque in the convent, we
did not know that Jacqueline Kennedy sat with her husband in
greasy spoons, as my mother would call coffee shops, talking to
farmers. Some days she boarded a private airplane, the *Caroline,*
and flew all around. Some days she was in Hyannis Port; other
days, Georgetown. She went to Times Square. She wrote her
"Campaign Wife" column. She wore fuchsia and ivory silk shan-
tung dresses, green wool suits, pillbox hats, overblouses, and
strings of pearls. She was not very much older than some of us
were.

In the usual silence of an ordinary November morning, 1960,
there was a piece of typing paper attached to the woodwork of
the door of the postulate. On it was printed in large letters, LAST
NIGHT JOHN F. KENNEDY WAS ELECTED PRESIDENT OF THE UNITED
STATES.

You felt at once that morning that you were more connected to
the United States. The handsome prince had kissed the institu-

tion of the presidency and had awakened her from her sleeping, secular state.

Jacqueline Kennedy had, for the inauguration, a sable muff. Diana Vreeland, who had dreamt up the muff, said as a kind of afterthought that "muffs are so romantic because they have to do with history."

I had a little muff when I was four or five, made of pure white fur. It had a string on it that went around my neck so I wouldn't lose it.

A Cat's Face

Our set, our group, was slightly diminished. We had begun to lose some of our fellow postulants.

A pew was empty at meditation and still empty at Mass. Was the person quite ill?

Or a chair was empty at dinner in the refectory. Perhaps the person had been asked to help serve.

Sometimes, then, at the end of Instructions, Sister C. would simply say that a certain postulant "had returned to her home."

I began to understand that the young women who left the convent were asked not to say anything to anyone. They disappeared. No one who was left knew—or no one appeared to know—anything about it.

I wondered what happened. It was all so mysterious. How had that person walked out without anyone seeing her?

Because I was so busy being perfect, I had seen my set not as individuals but as my set.

When a young woman went missing from our ranks, however, I was jolted out of what seemed a species of indifference. How could she have done this?

How did she feel, the one who left, that one who yesterday had been among us in silence, her face pure, her expression smooth and flat as a Burmese cat's? She could not or at least was instructed not to tell her story.

How long had she had doubts? Had she wrestled with them like Jacob with the angel, or had she simply said, "That's it"?

How had she felt when she'd shed that men's T-shirt we all wore, when she put on the white cotton blouse and checked skirt she'd worn to the convent? When she eased on her sheer beige nylons again, slipped on the calfskin black flats.

What did it feel like to walk out the door?

How many conversations had she had with the superior? Come to think of it, I'd thought I'd seen her talking to Sister C. in the Postulant Mistress's office twice in one week. What had Sister C. said? Had our former peer prayed? Did she think she was right to leave, or did she feel guilty?

And most important of all, I wondered: *Was* she right?

Or: Was she *right*?

But now she would not, could not, take the veil on February 2. She would never become a novice or a consecrated virgin.

Runes

When you became a bride of Christ, no human mediator intervened between the soul and Jesus. What could be better, purer, more dramatic? You would give your life directly to Christ and He would just have to love you back.

You wondered what He looked like.

. . .

When as a child I saw His face in framed pictures, I wasn't especially moved. The face never spoke to me, nor did the face on the
titanic mural painted on the concave space behind the altar at
Saint Luke's Church. Jesus was coming in a cloudy judgment in
this painting, his face not girlish but still bland and pale and flat as
in Eastern iconic paintings.

In high school I had begun to give up on what Christ looked
like, figuring it was hopeless, although I studied and studied the
shroud of Turin in photographs, trying to reconstruct the face
from the dark smudges on it. I saw it as grim, but that made
sense, because Jesus was dead by the time His face left its print.

I had been to many wakes and seen many people in open caskets, so I knew. I could have written poems about faces in caskets
but no one would have liked them.

When I heard the legend of Saint Veronica's veil, I sat up
straight in my grade school desk chair. Veronica had come forward while Jesus was carrying His cross and had wiped the blood
and sweat off His face with her veil. She must actually have blot-
ted His face rather than dabbed at it, because the veil is supposed
to have His features imprinted on it. Though at least a couple of
veils exist, the one purported to be the original is, according to
some sources, hidden away somewhere in Saint Peter's, Rome. I
once saw a photograph of what some think is the false veil.

In one sense these shrouds and veils suited me better than
any art I had seen. Jesus' face was better off blurry. Blurs,
like hieroglyphics, were mysterious and promising and hard to
decipher.

Later, in high school and college, as I began to put away the
things of a child, I stopped looking for Christ's literal face and
gave myself over to appreciating a new sense of Him in Hopkins's poems, which were, to a sixteen-year-old, like the shroud
and the veil, somewhat runic. Christ and God appeared strangely
in the poems side by side with oil and foil and smudges and

smears; with brinded cows, stallions, trout, and falcons; with rose-moles, eggs, ploughs, freckles.

I didn't know the definitions of some of the words Hopkins used. His difficult syntax, strung across enjambed lines, made me dizzy. Reading Hopkins felt like doing tumbling, which I was bad at, in gym class. But in this arena, maybe I could do my tumbling after all and maybe even become a professional acrobat.

> I am soft sift
> In an hourglass—at the wall
> Fast, but mined with a motion, a drift,
> And it crowds and it combs to the fall;
> I steady as a water in a well, to a poise, to a pane,
> But roped with, always, all the way down from the tall
> Fells or flanks of the voel, a vein
> Of the gospel proffer, a pressure, a principle, Christ's gift.

The Sister who taught you about Hopkins is, you know, a good teacher. You can't quite understand the subject matter.

But there is something, something. You want to know. You go to class, you discuss, you do your homework. Sister praises some, but not all, of your explications. You develop a certain taste for the difficulty of it. You sniff at it, nudge it with your nose. The very fact that the material keeps just ahead of you, is elusive, begins to intrigue you. The clear images keep you in the hunt.

Finally, you take big bites.

You may become anything after that; after that you may become even an eager animal, an Ibizan hound, say. Or an actual Egyptologist.

Because of this journal-writing, sketching, apparently tortured Roman Catholic English priest, my sense of poetry and my sense of God were changing. God and Christ and the Holy Spirit seemed less babyish and girlish: they began to seem oddly sophisticated and subtle. Could I relate to them that way? I thought so. And I could carry Father Hopkins's book of poems around; I could sit down and smoke, and read him: here were his lines, that novel rhythm, this sundered natural order of grammar, that shining new word.

It went something like: forget the visual, the soppy framed prints, gargantuan murals, the statues.

Words, the way Hopkins uses them, are better. And I had never known that a priest could have so many feelings.

No wonder his superiors looked askance.

Caroling in Advent

We were well into Advent, and Christmas was nearing. We began to celebrate the saints' feast days for December. On December 13, for example, we celebrated the feast of Saint Lucy, virgin and martyr, who chose death in the face of losing her virginity. Red vestments were worn on this day and the Introit began, *"Dilexisti justitiam et odisti iniquitatem."*

One evening the community was at prayer in the chapel when something strange happened. We heard singing—from outside the convent. I felt disoriented: music was coming from the outside in?

A group of people were singing Christmas carols. No nuns would do this. Not during Advent, a penitential season. Later, we were told that the singers were Clarke College students, who obviously weren't bothering with strict observances. But only the professed Sisters saw them; they were not allowed in to see the novices and the postulants.

Since I myself had been a Clarke College student, I guessed

that my pretty, smart roommate from Clarke was out there among the carolers in the winter evening.

I was reminded, then, that there was an actual outside peopled with young women who had no intentions of martyrdom or, though most of them were virgins, any intentions of becoming *consecrated* virgins. They were out there, out of doors, standing in the snow. I imagined what they might look like.

Maybe one of them had on a white angora beret and matching gloves. Someone else probably wore fleece-lined boots, the kind with which you did not need to wear shoes. (Another wouldn't be caught dead in boots and was freezing her feet wearing penny loafers with dimes in them.)

Angoras and fleeces. I had liked those fuzzy, textured, cloudlike materials.

After the caroling, if I had been with the Clarke students, I would probably have gone to downtown Dubuque for hot chocolate or coffee.

We would have said, "Why didn't our friends come to the windows?"

"One professed nun said they were 'busy.' I bet they weren't allowed."

"If we had gotten to see them, would you have told her that Jerry is drinking too much since she left him for the convent?"

"If she asked about him."

"I bet she wouldn't ask."

"I don't know. Finish your cigarette and let's go pack."

And then back to the dorm, Mary Frances Clarke Hall, to pack for Christmas vacation, which might mean a train ride home to Saint Paul or to Chicago. In addition to our suitcases, we had train cases—small and cordovan-colored, with set-in trays for our cosmetics—and we crammed them with Aqua Net, hairbrushes, coral and red lipsticks, Pretty Feet lotion, mascara and eyelash curlers, Amarige perfume, or maybe even My Sin.

. . .

On the train as a college student you could go to the dome car or the club car. You could have a toasted cheese sandwich and smooth your skirt and smoke and talk or play canasta. Then, finally, you stepped off the train at Saint Paul or Chicago into twenty degrees and swirling snow, and there were your parents to carry you off to dinner, where you had popovers and potatoes au gratin and frogs' legs and maybe even a Manhattan. And where there was a violinist and silver and red balls set on nests of holly. And ashtrays of green-tinted glass that said "Napoleon's" or "The London House" or "The Lexington" or "The Pump Room."

The caroling ended but we continued to sing, practicing a Gregorian chant. After that, after the ringing of the bell for the Solemn Silence, I was off to bed, off to my curtained alcove.

I tried not to think about Jerry. My imagined conversation about Jerry drinking too much, I knew, was true because Jerry had been *my* boyfriend freshman year at Clarke. He was the ex-G.I. who became despondent after I announced that I was going to become a nun.

And he had not seemed to get over it very fast; he had not gotten a new girlfriend whom he would marry and who would cook the veal for him. He drank instead.

Maybe if I had left him for some other fellow it would have been different and easier. Maybe my desire to become a nun was just too much for him.

Jerry would be all right in the end, I thought.

Nuns, I thought, especially younger ones, were often attractive but always forbidden and therefore that much more attractive. Nuns were in love with the Lord so that it stymied the men who happened to fall in love with them. It stymied the men so much that they consoled themselves the only way they could think of—by drinking, perhaps, at first, but then maybe by being good.

Some nuns understood this, I imagined, and felt their lives as much more interesting for it. They were the subjects of passions that would never flame out.

You had the Lord and you also had somewhere in your past a dejected-looking man who acted silly at first but who ultimately had changed his ways. If he did marry someone else, it was a huge compromise; he was really in love with you and always would be.

He was out there but he stayed put. He would never dare bother you. Mostly he chewed on a piece of straw or smoked and sometimes he sat and sometimes he stood up, at a place where the sky meets the sea on your distant horizon. He was a tiny figure at the edge of the nether blue.

Merry Christmas

Christmas Eve came. We went to bed as usual, but there would be a Midnight Mass. Would that terrible bell be set to waken us? We were told not to worry. I awoke to singing and to a thin, wavering light beyond my curtain.

It was a surprise. The novices had displaced the awful bell: already in their habits, they were processing through the dark halls, caroling. We, the surprised ones, dressed and went to the chapel, where the purple of Advent had given way to white altar cloths for Christmas. Poinsettias filled the sanctuary.

But not too many and not too few poinsettias. Here it was again: good taste. What I thought of as aesthetics to the bone. Was it something in the foundress's genes that set the tone for the BVMs forever? Or was it the present leadership?

.   .   .

Or perhaps it was the very approach to God the Beautiful that was the ringer. If you loved God and kept meditating on Him, did you eventually press something out of Him, absorb some secret thing from Him, some sense of proportion, clarity, balance, harmony, symmetry? And did that begin to show itself in how you decorated, how you knew that velvet ribbon, say, wide and the darkest of dark reds, tied onto something in a certain way, would make people happy so that they almost forgot to breathe?

In the convent, the decorating was simple, distinctive, pure, spare. It was much better than Christmas at home, where things were a jumble—my mother's Christmas candle collection, for instance.

When I was old enough to see over the top of our dining room table, there was a lake in its center. The lake must have been frozen, because snowmen candles stood on it and reindeer and angels. Before I could see the candles, I must have been able, like a little cat, to smell them.

Around the lake (a circular mirror) stood green tree candles frosted with white and Santa Clauses and carolers with red scarves swung over their shoulders, and choirboys. These last, the choirboys, had puffy cheeks and open mouths with lips drawn back, mysteriously formed, so that I could have sworn the candles were actually singing. The boys had little wax choir books resting on the open palms of their small beige hands, and red-orange cassocks and brown hair.

Each year my mother added to her candle collection so that it eventually overflowed the table to the surfaces of the buffet, the secretary, the coffee table, the gate-leg table. She overdid it, I thought.

My brother, Damon, and my father kept threatening to light them. "How about it?" one or another of them would say to my mother.

"What?"

"Let's light some of your candles."

"No."

"There are too many of them, anyway."

"Never mind."

"You never light any. They're candles. Let's light some."

"Don't you dare," Mother would say.

And we didn't.

Besides the candles, there was a blue-and-white tissue-paper shepherd scene to be fastened to our bay windows and then lit with a bulb from behind the cutout star. We had to wrestle it up, and some arguing went on about its placement.

We had New England clam chowder on Christmas Eve. Sometimes we cut ourselves on the white spun glass of our tree-top angel.

The Midnight Mass of my youth was so jammed that even if we got there half an hour early for pre-Mass caroling, we had to squeeze into some side pew. People would track snow in, which turned to slush, which turned to water. They would sing off-key, babies would cry or fall asleep, and the man behind me would smell of bourbon. The sermon would usually be homely and full of generalizations.

I could give up Christmas in the world, I had thought then, that Christmas with all its commercialism. It was almost a snap. At home in the world it was messy and various—too many Christmas candles overflowing a coffee table.

In the convent, all that was in bad taste seemed trimmed away: I never saw a frayed edge on the red velvet bows.

Joan of Arc's Kneecaps

Besides, January was coming. It was coming at me like the trains, the Burlington Zephyrs, I anticipated, with their dazzling center beams lighting up the tracks on dusky evenings. There was a rite ahead, the Rite of Reception into the religious life. February 2 would be the day. I would become a novice; though I wouldn't take any vows just yet, I would receive the habit.

We would be given new names, coupled with "Mary." Some Sisters in our order had what we thought of as women's names; some had men's names; some had double names associated with the same or different genders—Sister Mary Patrick David or Sister Mary Joan David.

I would become *Sister Mary Something* or *Sister Something Mary*. All the BVMs had been *Sister Mary Something* until the large numbers of young women joining meant that the community was running out of halfway reasonable names of either gender.

The new practice of allowing "Mary" to follow a name was thoughtful of our superiors because no one really wanted to be called Sister Mary Protase or Sister Mary Audifax or Sister Mary Smaragdus, even though these persons were actual canonized saints. Now there could be a Sister Mary Elizabeth and a Sister Elizabeth Mary.

We submitted three names of our own choosing after consulting the list of names of living BVMs. We would not know which name we would be given until the bishop pronounced it in public on February 2.

My first choice was Sister Mary Deborah, which, minus the "Sister," was the name my parents had bestowed on me. I liked it, except when an old priest in our parish who handed out report cards in grade school pronounced it "Deborah." But as I grew older I did not like what had happened to my name—it was shortened to Debby.

What was a Debby? I did not feel like a Debby—was the name somehow lacking the appropriate specific gravity? But no one would ever dare shorten a name I had been given in religion. I practiced writing it in longhand. Sister Mary Deborah. Sister Mary Deborah, BVM. The initials would identify my order—the Sisters of Charity of the Blessed Virgin Mary.

In those days when you had been a young woman out in the world, in certain delirious states you wrote other kinds of initials. You practiced writing your name as if you were your boyfriend's wife. In secret, you wrote "Mrs. Smith" and "Mrs. James Smith" again and again until it was perfect, until it nearly resembled anyone's handwriting but your own.

When as an infant I was baptized, the Catholic practice was that babies be given saints' names. But my sister and I had ended up with names from the Hebrew Bible: Judith and Deborah. My parents got around this by also naming each of us for Mary, the Virgin: Mary Judith and Mary Deborah. How could the priest say anything? This was daring. Was there some lingering resentment on my father's part because of the incident at his own baptism?

An old Czech priest who might as well have been the mayor of New Prague, Minnesota, because of all the power he had there in 1903, beheld my infant father being brought to baptism in his long, embroidered white dress. In Czech, he said, "What will you name this child?"

"Ralph," my grandmother said.

"Ralph!" he said. "What kind of name is that? No saint's name." And when the moment of pouring the water over the child's forehead came, he said, "Rudolph, I baptize you in the name of the Father and of the Son and of the Holy Ghost." But Ralph stood with my grandparents and with my father, who clearly enjoyed telling this story. And it stood legally. He lived in New Prague, Minnesota, but New Prague was in America, and in America he could be Ralph.

Besides Sister Mary Deborah, the other two names I had on my list were Sister Mary Saint Damian (after my brother) and Sister Joan Mary.

Toward the end of grade school, at the time of receiving the Sacrament of Confirmation, we had been allowed to choose another saint's name to add after our given name. And although I detested the hats they had ordered for us for Confirmation—white hats with brims and little insect pins on them to wear with our uniforms—and although I was frightened that the bishop might ask us questions as he routinely did to see if we had duly memorized the Baltimore Catechism, I bore something splendid away that day. The name of Joan of Arc. I became Mary Deborah Joan.

Joan of Arc was one of my heroines. And I liked the word "Arc."

Jeanne d'Arc. Virgin, martyr, holy warrior, chosen by God, unafraid to stand up to the hierarchy and tell the truth as she saw it. Saints Margaret and Catherine spoke directly to her. Not even being burned at the stake and being called a heretic could make her buckle, cave in. Of course, now the Church had itself recanted as to the way she was treated; otherwise, I don't know what view I would have had of her. I wanted to hear every version of every story about her. I pronounced the French names—my mother was part French—*dauphin, Rheims, Orléans.*

I studied any picture, any representation I could get of her. Joan listening to her "voices," to the saints talking to her. Joan leading the soldiers into war. Joan standing beside the dauphin as he, odd man, was being crowned. Joan being burned at the stake.

As I studied the clothes in the fashion magazines, so I studied the clothes of Joan in drawings. She wore armor. She wore pants. Her hair was cut short. Men respected her. They were her friends, but it was never sexual. She was pure in that way. Did she smoke? Did she ever have drinks with the soldiers? Roll dice with them and call them "you boys"?

She got to stay up late and make plans and pace back and forth. Had she ever sworn?

She had affected history. She, a woman, had intervened, had changed the course of things. She was poor, chaste, obedient. Well, obedient to her saints and thus to God.

This was better than being Cinderella. Better than Snow White, better than Rapunzel. Better than all those who often had things happen to them—being kissed by princes, for instance— that were thrilling but seldom had consequences for the whole world.

Being heroic, changing the world, was much better than being married and getting out the Electrolux, listening to the whine of that awful vacuum. Hearing the windows squeak as you washed them with ammonia and newspaper. Packing your six children's lunch pails and, worse, unpacking them. That nauseating, milky-thermos smell.

At the end, at the very end, at the stake when the flames were about as high as Joan's kneecaps, some priest, one of the execution party, heard the voices of Saints Margaret and Catherine talking to Joan. He thought, Oh, no.

Oh, no. Oh, God, she was right; she was telling the truth. And the priest called out loud, "I am burning a saint!"

I could stand being burned, I thought, if I changed the world in the process and then went to heaven after that. And think of how I would feel when I heard that poor priest shouting that I was a saint.

Then he would try in vain, that priest would, to smother the fire. For my part, I would, naturally, forgive him for having earlier put his torch to the kindling under my feet.

Even as I was dying, I would try to raise my voice and call to him.

"Écoutez! Écoutez: je vous pardonne. Non, non: ne pleurez pas!"

February 2, 1961, was upon us. It was the feast of the Purification, when in obedience to Mosaic Law, Mary took Jesus and presented herself at the temple. Candles would be blessed this day. I would become a nun.

PART TWO

Becoming a Novice

Hair and the Habit

On Reception Day, our new clothes, our nuns' habits, had been laid out on tables in a large classroom. At the proper point in the chapel ceremony we would process out, change, and process back in as Sisters.

We all had our hair quite short—but presentable—by now. Today, February 2, there would be no time-consuming cutting of hair during the robing in the classroom. Only in the next few days would we report to a given room and cut one another's hair to the quick, down to an inch or less.

Someone named Sister Margharita in *The Nun's Story* had said that the cutting off of hair was a sign of detachment since hair was "the chief adornment of women in the world." Monica Baldwin in *I Leap over the Wall* says flatly that her hair had been cropped "convict-wise."

But it was in the film version of *The Nun's Story* that the hair-cutting seemed most impressive. The shears had blades that looked long and sharp and competent, and Sister Luke's / Audrey Hepburn's locks were thick and dark and were cut away in clumps so solid that they almost thumped when they landed on the tray. It had looked like a real sacrifice.

❧

In her anger she clutched Rapunzel's beautiful tresses, wrapped them twice around her left hand, seized a pair of scissors with the right, and snip, snap, they were cut off and the lovely braids lay on the ground.

※

The modern managing of postulants' hair seemed rather colorless, I thought, compared to what had once been. Most of us had worn our hair short when we were in the world, anyway. I had.

Our vesture, the actual putting on of our new clothing, would take little time for we had practiced a day or so before our Reception. The black serge skirt remained the same. Things on top had grown more complicated.

We had wide half sleeves that snapped onto our blouses and that were to be worn over the close-fitting inner sleeve. This business of the sleeves, once I manipulated and twisted everything into place, struck me as truly medieval or Renaissance, right out of some of the movies I'd seen, although no Richard Burton or Peter O'Toole would ever be taking the hand that belonged to my sleeved arm and putting his lips to it. We would still wear black waist-length capes but the white collar changed—it was sturdier, even more starched in effect, and had tiny pleats or scorings in it, like faille.

The headdress was tricky; it consisted of a sort of net-and-cotton skullcap, a hood, and a veil. The skullcap, flat to begin with, had long tabs so that I could place it on my head, cover part of my forehead with the solid fabric, and pin the tabs at the back with small white hat pins. The hood, scored and starched, with the veil pinned to it with black hat pins, also had tabs at the back that attached to the skullcap.

The veil fell straight past my shoulders and down my side and my back to about my hips.

If you had had any hips of which you were aware in those days.

You had no shoulders, no side, no back, no hips. No elbows,

no little toes, no calves, no ankles. You knew you had a head: all that headgear had to be attached to something.

Of course, you did have a head. You mostly thought and you reasoned. You saw and you heard and you talked by means of your head, also. Or you refrained from talking when you were silent. You were positive you had a head.

We Become Nuns

Still dressed as postulants, we knelt, row after row of us, in turn, at the communion rail. The bishop moved along the railing.

"I receive you into the Congregation of the Sisters of Charity of the Blessed Virgin Mary. Your name in religion will be ————." When he reached me, he said these words of reception and then, "Your name in religion will be Sister Mary Deborah."

Oh, I thought. Good. And no more Debbys ever again.

I listened for the naming of the others. Tessa retained her name as well: Teresa.

The ceremony continued in the chapel while we processed out for our vesting. Some of the senior novices also left the service to help us dress. Each one of us went to a station in the classroom and began putting on our new cape and collar, headdress, and the white veil of the novice. In addition, there was a leather belt with a long, large rosary and crucifix attached to it, and this was fastened around the waist.

We did not speak. We tried not to look; we tried not to break custody of the eyes. I only partly succeeded and when I glanced up once, I saw Tessa in her habit, standing there, and she was transformed, shining as if she were backlit.

We came back through the doors of the chapel in procession

to the sound of the organ and the unearthly singing of the schola, that group composed of the best singers from the already select group of the choir.

There were suddenly no postulants in that chapel.

We were novices; we were nuns; and I was Sister Mary Deborah.

The superior rang the bell for recreation at breakfast that morning, a special treat for the day of our reception into religious life. We could talk while enjoying our wieners and sweet rolls.

The Nose

We spoke at Reception Day breakfast. But the first sounds that rose from the refectory tables took the shape of *oh-h-hs*.

Oh-h-hs went up like smoke rings.

It was pure *The Nun's Story* now. After the vesture in the Belgian convent, Gabrielle, Gaby, who is about to become Sister Luke, thinks that all of them look alike—"like angels slightly surprised." Part of her Sisters' startlement came from the fact that their view was obstructed by their headdresses, but our own BVM habit had been revised so that the old, squared, forward thrust of the coif—said to remind the Sisters of their coffins—had given way to a simple hood. Some of the Sisters had started driving and needed to see out to the side. No custody of the eyes while they were driving.

Our own surprise was fueled, then, by the unobstructed view of one another. During breakfast, one of my Sisters—now they were my *Sisters*—made a remark to me from across the table. "Some people," she said, "look more beautiful in the habit than they did before the habit. You," she continued, "are one of them. You look just beautiful."

I did?

She sounded like Sister Luke's elderly infirmary patients, who at night, when she reported for nursing duty, turned on all their call bells at once in order to see her in her new habit. "How beautiful you are, Sister!" they said.

I did not know what to say. The remark was flatly personal, the most personal comment anyone had made to me in a long time, for my Saint Paul friends had stopped making them. On top of that, the person who had said it was the one who had eyes like Orson Welles's. I remember being happy about her comment, but what was I supposed to do with looking beautiful when I was in a convent, entering into the life and mind-set of a nun?

People's remarks to me about Jackie Kennedy dated from my taking of the veil. "You look like Jackie Kennedy." I did? How could that be? I didn't look like Jackie Kennedy before I was a nun, and now I did?

It was the veil that did it, I decided. My short hair was replaced by an odd equivalent of long hair—the veil—and that made me look different. Prettier?

"It's your nose," my sister, Judy, said eventually. "In profile, it's just like hers."

My nose? Not my new, fabricated hair? Maybe people looked at my face, at my nose more, because everything else except my hands and a small part of my neck was covered.

Nightcap

Another item was part of our wardrobe from the date of our becoming novices. A nightcap.

Lying folded and flat on a table, it looked like a simplified, shrunken bonnet with no strings. It was cream-colored, with my identifying community number, 4,000-something, neatly stitched in red on the back lower edge.

Why did we wear it, besides its being a tradition? Not for warmth—we didn't wear the nightcaps in bed. The obvious answer was that our hair was so short.

But why did we wear it? Our hair was pretty short when we were postulants, too.

After we reported for our first really short haircuts, I knew why. None of us looked too beautiful, I thought, with near crew-cuts. No Jackie Kennedys were anywhere in sight. When a sleepy novice forgot at night to wear her nightcap to the bathroom, it wasn't pretty. Did the community, with its inherited sense of aesthetics, realize this? Otherwise, the ones who had done away with the huge, square "coffin" coif would have done away with the nightcap.

Thank God for what I now had, then: the cap at night and the daytime veil that mimicked long hair and fell to my shoulders and fell down my back and never needed setting and never needed straightening and never needed peroxide and required no spray net.

On Straight

On the day after our reception into the community, on February 3, we would celebrate the feast of Saint Blaise, bishop and martyr. Our chaplain would wear red vestments.

Saint Blaise was an Armenian bishop who was ripped by wool combs and then beheaded during the persecutions of the Roman emperor Licinius. He is said to have saved a boy with a fish bone stuck in his throat from choking to death. He blessed the boy's throat and thereby dissolved the bone.

He is also said to have convinced a wolf to let go of a pig that belonged to a poor woman. He is the patron saint of those with throat diseases, of wild animals, and of wool combers.

Per intercessionem S. Blasii, liberet te Deus a malo gutteris et a quovis alio malo. . . .

On February 3, out in the world and everywhere, two blessed unlit candles—since that woman who got her pig back brought candles to Blaise when he was in jail—are crossed so that they look like an X. The priest, moving along the communion rail, where his faithful are kneeling, would hold for a moment the point of one of the V's of that X lightly against a person's neck, and pray.

The rising prayer on February 3 was the same as always, but that morning I was a nun, and for the second time in my life putting on the dress of a nun. I worried that I would not be able to get it right—all the rigors, the straight pins with their black-and-white heads, all the tapes, the snaps, the adjustments—and get to the chapel for morning prayers and Mass, although we had been given more time that first morning. I wanted the netted-and-solid-fabric skullcap on right, and I wanted my hood to be on perfectly straight.

Was this vanity? Perfectionism? And how to distinguish perfectionism, attention to the aesthetics of donning a nun's garb, from a sanctioned striving, in all humility, to be perfect? To be perfect was of the essence of the Holy Rule. It was at the heart of dedication to God, after all, wasn't it?

I got to my pew on time, with everything on straight.

Once a young man I had dated told me that he dreamed he was walking behind me and that the seams of my nylons were not in fact straight; they were quite crooked. This time the boy was not the psychiatrist's son—but he might as well have been. Or a prophet's son.

Had he not had a deep insight? For I wanted everything straight. Perhaps he knew what I sometimes feared: I might have a crooked self.

Friendship Again

We immediately began our canonical year, a "junior novice" year in which we would forsake secular studies for sacred ones: scripture, canon law, various courses in theology, and regular morning Instructions in the religious life given by a Novice Mistress. No history, biology, literature for a year. How many women in the whole world, I thought, have something this good, this crisp-sounding and focused and intellectual, and at the same time this God-oriented? A canonical year.

We would devote ourselves to examining the things of God, the things of the supernatural, the things of the Church. And we would be engaged in domestic work as well.

One of the rules that we now examined in more depth was

that one which inveighed against the particular friendship. This time I noticed that the Constitutions went beyond a simple ban on singular friendships. They also said that if there were "particular friendships," then in a short time the whole community could be "overthrown."

I puzzled over this and then decided it must mean that there could be factions; that people could conspire together, that mutual charity, not to speak of obedience, would be on the skids. No doubt this notion of the whole community being overthrown—something unimaginable to me—attested to the dangerousness of the "Particular Friendship" (though the words were not capitalized in the rule item, they were forever capitalized in my mind).

The proscription, whatever the explicit rationale, had several implicit intents and various effects. It meant that everyone felt more or less included. There was no one in our set who needed to worry ever again that others would get the psychological equivalents of valentines and she wouldn't get a single one.

The blow to friendships cost some of us more obviously than others. Some knew they had special friends, even though they didn't call it a friendship and even though they complied with the rule by not seeking certain people out all the time. A warmth sprang up here and there between one person and another.

I wanted to get to know people better, but in those days did the opposite of trying. I sensed high spirits and humor and indefatigable friendliness in Jane, who tried to contain herself but was not always successful. She blushed a great deal—at everything that happened. I wanted to get to know her but I was still too busy being perfect and centering all my hopes on God.

Some of us kept ourselves, either by fidelity to the rules or by means of our natural dispositions, as far away as possible from appreciating affinities between ourselves and another person. We appeared to manage.

· · ·

From your childhood, depending on your makeup, you were salty about religious rules or you weren't. You bound yourself with them, or you shucked and shrugged them off, or you fell somewhere in between. You asked questions out loud or silently or you didn't ask them at all or you asked them once in a while. You stomped out and regretted it or you didn't give a darn. You stood still and fumed or you cheerfully stood still. You were sanguine or choleric or phlegmatic or bilious about rules, or you were some or all of these by turn. Some parents were the models for the way you ended up responding; some were not.

But what about the sexual issues underlying the rule against friendship? Or rather, the fear of them? For I was sure there must be fear somewhere in the background.

I never saw any physical, intimate, sexual contact between two nuns. But because of something I noticed one day—a gaze—it did occur to me, if only vaguely, that such a thing could happen.

A Gaze

After my duties one morning, I walked into a kind of cloakroom where the novices hung their blue work aprons. Two of my set stood inside, stood quite close to each other. They talked a bit, which, according to the rule, would have been occurring only because it was necessary. But I thought that this conversation lacked the character of necessity. They appeared to be gazing into each other's eyes. Something about this was odd. It put me off my stride.

Their stances and the way they were looking at each other:

these were the stances and the looks of lovers. I could only guess that it was an attraction, perhaps some kind of erotic attraction.

One of the two nuns could, actually, have played the part of Romeo well; the other had a sort of sweet Southern belle cast to her. As in a tragedy, there would have been grave obstacles to the relationship: in this case, the superiors as the ever-watchful Capulets and Montagues.

I wondered: could such obstacles plus the pressures of religious life plus the absence of men actually fuel romances in the convent? I didn't know. Whatever the case, I was convinced it would never lead anywhere, would never lead to serious intimacies. Most of us barely knew how men and women made love, much less—and we didn't want to think about it—women and women.

I figured it was some kind of infatuation.

I knew that crushes and infatuations were not always bad. I had had some crushes in my time and others had had them on me.

Sometimes crushes were funny. At church camp during the summer I turned twelve, a ten-year-old tent mate said to me: "I like the way you make your cot up in the morning."

Oh. Nice of her to say so. "You do?"

"Yes. I like the way you do everything."

What *was* this? "You do?"

"Yes. I like the way you work on your raffia bracelet during crafts time. I like the colors you choose, too."

Good grief.

"I like the way you brush your teeth," she said. "I like the way you spit in the basin."

Raw Eggs, a Green Sweater, and Ham

My domestic assignments during the canonical year included being a kitchen novice, an icebox novice, and a special assignment serving novice.

The kitchen and meal-duty novices worked on the ground level, or lowest floor, of the convent. Three great ranges, side by side, dominated the expansive kitchen with its long, dazzling stainless steel counters. I worked under the tutelage of a practical-minded, wry professed Sister, Sister K. She swallowed two raw eggs every morning for her health.

Just like Sister Luke! She had taken them during the days of her tuberculosis cure in the Congo. Dr. Fortunati, the surgeon whom she assisted in the operating theater, had brought the raw egg yolks—which he called "oysters on the prairie"—to her in crystal wineglasses. He had brought not two egg yolks in *one* wineglass, but one egg yolk in *each* wineglass, and he had sprinkled them with a little parsley and lemon juice.

He saw her staring at the wine glasses used only for visits of high personages.

"Presentation is everything to a TB, Sister," he said smiling. "You should know that."

I thought this comment of his was unbeatable. No wonder I had been in love with Dr. Fortunati. That man, even though he had a sardonic side, was just so sophisticated that he gave me the shivers. He would walk through a door humming an air from *Tosca.*

And in that remark by Dr. Fortunati, between what he *said*

and his *smiling*, in Kathryn Hulme's sentence there was, brilliantly, no comma.

Sister K. would be waiting for us in the lower depths to which we designated kitchen novices would descend after studying scripture or the BVM Constitutions or canon law for hours at a stretch.

Without any transition then, our heads full of the language of exegesis or of the status of moral persons or of the perils of particular friendship, we began to heat pans and fry pork chops for around three hundred people for the main meal of the day. The ranges had multiple burners on them and as many as four of us would wield the massive wrought iron frying pans, cooking and turning the pork chops for as long as it took.

Sister K. commented from time to time. She called everyone "Mary" or "dearie."

"That's too much sugar, Mary."

"No, dearie, not that way."

"Look at that, Mary, that's burny. That pork chop's burny. You don't want to get it that dark." Somehow you didn't mind when she criticized your technique. It was never personal—you were a Mary and your Sisters had to be fed, and moreover your Sisters had to be fed decently prepared food.

My sojourn in these regions was a bright stew of warmth, lights overhead, and occasions for fairly necessary talk and for the amusement that often accompanies cooking. I felt a little more human; I bent a little amid all these sensory experiences; I felt happy under the eye of the comedic, good-hearted Sister K.

Range burners glowed Pompeian red when we fried or boiled potatoes. We worked at the shining counters over fifty limpid pie crusts, filling them with sliced apples, butter, sugar, and cinnamon. Sister K. swallowed her raw eggs and moved about her kitchen—no doubt, this was *her* kitchen, whether in the spirit of poverty she thought so or not. In one corner, the dish-washing novices scratched at huge dirty pans and bumped them from deep sink to drainboard. Novices came down from the Bake House looking like phantoms with their floured faces and hands.

Part of my duty involved taking care of the food in two walk-in iceboxes and one freezer in a room that lay just off the vegetable-peeling room. A green sweater, of all things, hung in this room. It was, I was told, for me to wear when I rummaged around in the iceboxes; otherwise, I would get too cold and might indeed even *get* a cold.

Why wasn't the sweater black or white? Even though it seemed a little wicked, the green sweater did, I liked it. It set me off; no one else in the whole place wore green or any other color. I looked forward to wearing it while I was in the iceboxes studying jars of peaches for signs of spoilage, counting packages of wieners and packages of sliced ham, shifting cans of milk.

For several months my appointment also consisted of being server to "The Boys."

The Boys were groundskeepers and maintenance men and they were gray-headed and seemed to me to all be in their sixties. One of my fellow servers said at recreation one day that one or more of them had done some allegedly wicked things as young men but that they had reformed and were working for the nuns to make up for whatever sins they had committed.

Father Vermeuhlen

Of course: The Boys were a version of my Father Vermeuhlen from *The Nun's Story*. Father Vermeuhlen, as a missionary in the African bush, out of a desperate loneliness, had lived with a Bantu woman and had had three children by her. Later, after delivering the children for their education to an order of nuns, he disappeared back into the bush, headed in the opposite direction of his original mission.

He eventually went to Rome, repented, and received his Sacred Orders, his priestly faculties, back. As a penance for his sins, he returned to Africa to work in a leper colony, where he was much beloved. We do not know what happened to his consort, the Bantu woman, when she found that he had gone forever from her side. And what of her children?

Father Vermeuhlen had appeared in my life now in the form of the purportedly sinful Boys.

And there was someone else—how could I have forgotten! My uncle Roman, who had, sadly, just died.

The Castaway

Uncle Roman—what must my grandmother have had in her head to name her American children Cleopha, Roman, and Consuelo? I speculated. Mary of Cleophas, according to Saint John, had stood at the foot of the cross; our Church was the Church of Rome; "Consuelo," though, had Spanish roots—it suggested consolation. Still, none of my friends' relatives had odd names like these.

Uncle Roman had been what we called a terror. As a teenager he had been expelled from his Catholic boys' school, Saint Thomas, for swearing at one of the priest-teachers. When my grandmother Peil went to the archbishop of Saint Paul and begged him to ask the academy to take Roman back, she had gotten down on her knees. Roman went back.

Dark-haired, he was movie-star handsome—no, even *more* handsome than Cary Grant, than Clark Gable, than Gregory

Peck. His facial features were perfectly regular. "He loved the girls," my mother said. But Mary Peil had other plans for her son: he would be a priest. In Saint Paul, the priests were the powerful ones.

Uncle Roman did not want to be a priest. But he entered the Saint Paul Seminary and was eventually ordained.

Then there began a series of incidents about which I was not told much. Roman became a navy chaplain and, while serving on a battleship, ran up gambling debts. That fascinated me. The vision of a relative of mine, a priest—his black hair and intelligent eyes set off even more by the white of his chaplain's uniform—gambling on the high seas, was beyond belief. If it had not been so truly awful, I thought, it would have been a little thrilling.

Later, he was transferred out of our archdiocese to someplace in North Dakota; I took it that this was a punishment of some kind. Still later, he was assigned to a church in the archdiocese of New York. How unlikely that one of our relatives—practically all Minnesotans—should actually have lived for a time in Manhattan, among the brownstones.

In New York City, my mother told me, he had fallen in love with a blond parishioner whose name was Irene. And the two of them had simply disappeared then. They had run off together and had not been heard from again.

Mother's brother was lost to her until a night about thirty years later when the telephone rang at our house and it was Uncle Roman, who was in Greensboro, North Carolina. "Connie," he said to my mother, "I've buried Irene." Only after the woman he loved died did he feel he could perhaps rejoin his family and the Church.

Mother often used to call something that happened a "gift from heaven." When I came home from college freshman year, she said, "Your being here is like a gift from heaven." *Who, me?* I thought. Sometimes I had been cranky and thoughtless toward her. Then she said, "Go look in your room. It looks nice and I put some cigarettes on your dresser for you." The new package was lying inside a sparkling ashtray; it had been carefully opened and one cigarette pulled out in an inviting way. The way I imagined the Waldorf-Astoria would have done it.

Uncle Roman's telephoning, his materializing after all those years, was another one of her gifts from heaven, she said. After all he'd done? She didn't appear to be ashamed. He was her brother.

This was how we ended up in North Carolina in 1960, just months before I was to enter the convent. Uncle Roman and Irene had gone south from New York City.

Once you jumped the ship of the Church you could best lose yourself in the South, I guessed. Once in a while—maybe—you could forget you were a castaway. His move told me that he, at least, had been ashamed of what he had done. That made two of us.

He had worked wherever he could; he sold vacuum cleaners in Memphis, pitched insurance in Greensboro. He changed his name to Michael, which had been my grandfather Peil's name.

I studied him in his modest house. I watched him drink Fleischmann's whiskey, my parents' favorite. He was no longer handsome, which I thought seemed fitting. His hair was white; he had a gray mustache. He looked like any other old man.

He drank and he drank. He's an alcoholic, I thought.

He told us he was sorry for all he had done. He wanted to do penance.

I spoke to him when he spoke to me, but I couldn't stand him. Let's get out of here, I thought. Let's get back in the car, where my mother can read her book in the backseat while I sit in the front seat and work on the argyle socks I am knitting or scan the black and blue and red threads of the highways on road maps so I can tell my father what the next town was and precisely how far it would be between the circled dots.

When we left Greensboro we were going to New York. I

planned to have a Manhattan in the hotel bar there: *She had a Manhattan in Manhattan the summer she entered the convent.*

In Uncle Roman's or Michael's—or whoever in the world he was—kitchen I found myself staring at the shiny crimson smudges on an old stove. He saw me staring. Before Irene had died, he explained, she had started going blind, so he had taken nail polish and daubed it near critical points on the stove dials. Irene could see where "ON" was for the oven: just turn the dial so it matched the big red bloom of nail polish. She could see where "350" was: another nail polish daub flowered there.

She may have liked to cook? I checked the question I was about to ask. I reminded myself: what did *that* matter, that she cooked? What difference did cooking meals for someone make? She had lived in sin.

On a side table in the living room was a framed picture of her, and rarely had I seen anyone so lovely. She had light hair; she reminded me of June Allyson. I had wanted her to be—what? Sordid-looking. This whole thing is just awful, I thought. What is he doing with a picture of her right out in the open like that if he's so sorry?

Again I thought: Let's get out of here. If I had been able to use the word "hell," I would have thought, Let's get the hell out of here. Right now.

My mother and father slept in a trundle bed in Uncle Roman's spare bedroom and I slept with them, on an old mattress. In the middle of the second night we were there, after my parents and Michael/Roman had spent the evening with their Fleischmann's highballs, a crash awakened me. My mother and I sat up. My father slept on.

"Ralph," my mother said and pushed hard on my father's back. Before he could roll over, another crash. It sounded like someone was throwing small tables, small chairs against a wall.

"What's that?" my father said.

My mother said, "It's Roman."

He was drunk, stumbling drunk, plunging around in his bedroom. *"God,"* he shouted, and I winced. *"God!"*

It seemed it would all work out, though, in the end. My aunt, his other sister, Sister Mary Cleopha, knew of a rehabilitation center for wayward and alcoholic priests in Jemez Springs, New Mexico. It was run by a religious order of men called the Servants of the Paraclete. Roman could go there and be rehabilitated, which sounded good to me. "Rehabilitated" was a good word.

Would he want to go there?

He would.

My mother sent him money to help with the move.

I entered the convent and Roman went to Jemez Springs. He stopped drinking and applied to Rome to receive his Sacred Orders back so that he could say Mass within the Church again. He wrote me letters saying he would join the Servants of the Paraclete, the good men who were caring for him. He became a novice about the same time I did.

I had begun to feel kindly toward him.

He sent pictures. My uncle Roman was living not far from Santa Fe, in a blue-gray habit and looking handsome again, cutting a striking figure against a broad New Mexico sky. If a person could lose himself in the South, he could perhaps find himself in the West. How strangely things worked out.

Oddly, he wrote me about how he loved doing dishes with the other Servants, his brothers in Christ. He talked about picking up the dish towel and drying away and joking (didn't, I wondered, they have a rule of silence there?). He dried the clunky plates and cups and he dried the heavy soup bowls, and his joy, apparently, was full.

And now he was dead of a heart attack just as his Sacred Orders were arriving from Rome. So he was buried, according to the custom then for priests, with the chalice he would have used to say Mass had he not died. Any Masses he would have said before reinstatement by Rome would have been valid—because

once a priest, always a priest—but not really licit. I was so proud
of him now that grieving seemed beside the point.

Was my uncle Roman's story after all any less shocking
than Father Vermeuhlen's? The battleship, New York City,
Greensboro, and Jemez Springs all amounted to the African
bush as far as I was concerned. Oh, these *priests,* I thought.
These men.

Burny

The Boys, the six of them, usually wearing faded plaid shirts with
the sleeves rolled up, entered the lower hallways from a side door
of the convent and went directly to the small dining room that
was exclusively for their use. They appeared for breakfast, dinner,
and supper. They talked. They mostly ate.

Two of us served, bringing them bowls of potatoes, mashed
rutabagas, platters of ham and roast beef. Coffee, milk, water,
iced tea. Desserts—bread pudding, apple pie. Bacon and eggs for
breakfast. No wieners.

The first time we served, one of The Boys looked at us and
said to the air as we left the room, "New ones."

As soon as we served them, we withdrew. Then after a time
we reappeared to see if they wanted seconds. They always did.

Sometimes they talked. One of them made funny remarks
and he looked at me when he did so. He knew we servers should
not speak unless it was necessary, so sometimes he asked us questions that seemed pertinent to the food we were serving, but
which really were not. We answered.

The Boys duty was my favorite duty of all.

One day, after morning Instructions in the novitiate, Sister K.

summoned all of us—cooks and servers—to the head of one of the steel tables in the kitchen. In front of her sat a platter with a few strips of very dark bacon on it.

"Now," Sister K. said, "Sisters, just look at that."

We looked.

"What do you see?"

"Bacon, Sister," someone said.

"What kind of bacon, Mary?"

"Well, it is overcooked."

"It's more than overcooked, Mary," Sister K. said. "It's burny, now isn't it?"

"Yes, Sister."

"Yes. Now," she continued, "would you serve this bacon to Mother Mary T., our Mother General?"

"Oh no," one of us said, and we all shook our heads, *oh no.*

"*No,* and if you would not serve this bacon to Mother Mary T., our Mother General, then why would any one of you have served it to The Boys?"

She paused and looked at each one of us. Then she said, "Which you did."

A Keyhole

We studied the Old Testament in the Douay-Rheims version of the Bible, which many of us had never read all the way through. Eventually, we came to Solomon's Canticle of Canticles, also referred to as the Song of Songs.

> Let him kiss me with the kiss of his mouth; for thy breasts are better than wine,

Smelling sweet of the best ointments. Thy name is as oil poured out: therefore young maidens have loved thee.

. . . .

A bundle of myrrh is my beloved to me, he shall abide between my breasts.

A cluster of cypress my love is to me, in the vineyards of the Engaddi.

Behold thou art fair, O my love, behold thou art fair, thy eyes are as those of doves.

Behold thou art fair, my beloved, and comely. Our bed is flourishing.

. . . .

I am the flower of the field, and the lily of the valleys.

As the lily among thorns, so is my love among the daughters.

As the apple tree among the trees of the woods, so is my beloved among the sons. I sat down under his shadow, whom I desired: and his fruit was sweet to my palate.

He brought me into the cellar of wine, he set in order charity in me.

Stay me up with flowers, compass me about with apples: because I languish with love.

His left hand is under my head, and his right hand shall embrace me.

The Church certainly had a vast language: we had come from the juridical persons and the divine dispositions of canon law to this.

The Canticle of Canticles, we were taught, has to do with typology; that is, the bride and the groom in these texts are figural or prefigural types of Christ and the Church. What a grand idea.

If others in my class felt as I did, they were grateful that the explanation of typology was handed to us, that we were given a way to abstract all those bellies of white ivory, those grape-cluster breasts, the legs, navels, and mouths; all that myrrh and dripping honey, all those beds of spices.

It was nice that even though we were to be brides of Christ, the type of the bride here was not us, but us once removed—that is, the Church. Had the bride been us, it would have been a little too close for comfort, although I loved the part where the groom was calling, "Rise up, my love, my dove, my beautiful one, and come away." He was inviting the loved one into the spring land-scape where the turtledove sang.

Typology or not, I got a little nervous when I read on:

> I sleep, and my heart watcheth; the voice of my
> beloved knocking: Open to me, my sister, my love,
> my dove, my undefiled: for my head is full of dew,
> and my locks of the drops of the night.
> I have put off my garment, how shall I put it on?
> I have washed my feet, how shall I defile them?
> My beloved put his hand through the keyhole, and
> my bowels were moved at his touch.

The groom was not only poking about the keyhole to the bride's room; he was putting his hand through it. Better not to dwell on this, I thought; set it aside and read the commentary.

Without the literary concept of typology, would this book have been on the Catholic Church's *Index of Forbidden Books*?

No, They Don't

Somehow, oddly, a rumor had arisen. Someone told me that she had heard a rumor about the senior novices. She got right to the point. "I heard that they tell their faults out loud."

"What?"

"Every week they tell their faults out loud. In front of Sister Y., who gives them a penance. On Friday afternoons."

"No, they *don't*."

"Yes, they do. The whole session is called the Chapter of Faults."

I had noticed that every Friday afternoon around four, the senior novices went to the senior novice classroom, closed the doors, and stayed put for about an hour.

All I could say was, "But we tell our faults in confession."

"Those are the sins. Not the faults that are infractions against the rule."

How would I be able to bear this? At least in confession, I felt embarrassed only in front of the priest. This must be the place, I thought; finally we come to the place where nuns *prostrate* themselves; I imagined the senior novices lying facedown on the floor, at the same time trying to project their voices as they enumerated their faults. If my Sister Luke had done this, I had forgotten it or dismissed it as medieval, archaic. Iowa was not Belgium.

This was a specter. Not only would I have to tell my faults, I would have to go through the same process I went through for confession. Now it would be twice a week, in different contexts. Remember the faults and the sins, tell them correctly—not too vague, not too detailed—and do not be proud of what will appear as an honest, humble recital.

. . .

In addition, and almost the worst of all, would be those times when you could not think of a rule you had broken. What would you say in the Chapter of Faults, then? Would you make something up? Otherwise, it would sound as if you thought you were perfect.

And then I thought how terrible it was that I should feel daunted by and frightened of the Chapter of Faults. How terrible that I should have that feeling. By means of the Great Chain of Being in place precisely because of my vocation, the Chapter was manifestly the Will of God for me. Therefore, I should embrace it.

Besides, maybe it would be the same for me as after confession, when I felt like I was floating because all the weight of my sins had been lifted. The confessional up to now had been like a bath and afterward I felt clean. I tried to look on the bright side. Now there would be two baths.

The Chapter of Faults

It was indeed called the Chapter of Faults, an old monastic custom, and it was legislated by the community. Within the Chapter, the nuns proclaimed their faults out loud. Someone would tell of how she had broken the rule of silence unnecessarily or of how she had begun to seek the same person out at recreation time and again. Penances were distributed by the superior. Each one of the Sisters knew, then, how well every one of the other Sisters was or was not keeping the Holy Rule.

The Chapter of Faults could actually be found right there in the 1958 BVM Constitutions in a section we had not yet studied, entitled "Other Exercises of Piety." The Chapter would be

> held twice a month throughout the entire school year. The accusation of faults is limited to external transgressions of the Constitutions. The penance to be imposed in the chapter of faults should be opportunely moderated by the spirit of discretion.

Why, though, hadn't they told us about this? It seemed like some kind of breach of full disclosure.

In the end, by what seemed like a miracle, we were spared the Chapter of Faults. The Council of the community ended it just as we were to start the second year of our novitiate. Evidently, the leadership had found the practice archaic. When the Novice Mistress announced its demise to us, the room grew even stiller than it had been.

This was but the beginning of many such abolishments and transformations. We were making history. We were a set on the cusp of change of things religious.

A Cup Handle

We were drying dishes one day after dinner and I was thinking of Uncle Roman, who had loved drying in Jemez Springs, when a handle from one of our serviceable tan-colored cups came off in my hands.

I knew I must go to my superior. Any breakage, any destruction of an object, must in the spirit of poverty be reported.

"How did you do that, Sister?"

"I was drying a cup and the handle came off in my hands, Sister." I hesitated. I realized I had made it sound as if it had just happened, as if I had not mishandled the cup. *Had* I mishandled it? Had I been too vigorous? It was hard to say.

Then a corner of the wide, severe mouth on Sister D.'s gaunt face turned up just a bit. Was it a grimace, or a watery smile, a flicker of a smile? "All right, Sister," she said.

All right? I had expected a small penance.

"And Sister, please, in the future, try to refrain from crushing our cups."

So it had been a smile. The reportage of a mere cup handle had been a little too much even for her, this woman whom my Sister Luke would have called a Living Rule.

Carefully, I smiled back at her.

A superior had let her guard down. She had looked right at me as if I were a person and had responded to me with a little sympathy, with a humor that came close to warmth.

On reflection, that I was so pleased by this appalled me. It was a pittance that she had dealt out and I took it as generous and comforting. Still, it was a spectacular emotional exchange compared to—what? Well, compared to no emotional exchanges.

No Touching

In fact, in months and months no one had touched me, except when with others I turned up every two or three months to get the equivalent of a buzz cut from a fellow novice.

I never touched anyone.

I touched my own skin with my fingers only when I washed my hands and shampooed my short hair; in the shower or bathtub, I used a washcloth for the rest of my body. I had loved warm bathwater, but one superior had warned us about lingering in the bathtub—that it made you somehow slack.

I could not pet a dog or a cat or the head of a canary or the back of a tiny turtle.

The fabrics I did touch were black and white serge, wool, cotton. There was no crushed velvet, no fleece, no angora, and no slubbed silk.

I had worn something knitted for a while, though. That green sweater I had worn for my icebox patrols. I missed it when my duty changed. Putting on a knit had somehow been so comforting. It had texture.

Impure That Way

The vicissitudes of touch were over, and that brought some relief. If someone said "touch," I always thought *impure*.

"Impure" came up in elementary school and we knew it had to do with the sexual. There were impure thoughts, impure words, and impure deeds, and they were all sins.

Once, a shopkeeper who knew little English had tried to explain that a T-shirt I was considering buying would not shrink. "Pure," he said, taking the shirt in his hands and yanking it, stretching it on the horizontal. "Pure this way." Now he yanked and stretched it on the vertical. "Pure that way." He set the shirt down. "Pure all ways. Pure, pure."

For us, as young Catholics, it was impure this way. Whichever way we turned, impure was lurking. Impure that way. Impure, impure.

· · ·

Impure touches fell under impure deeds. It meant, the nuns said, touching a part of someone's body or your own body where you shouldn't be touching it. Who in the world would want to touch oneself or a boy in the wrong place anyway? Touch a grade school boy on his body? Boys were mostly thin and flat, like 3M products—why would you want to touch them? What was there to touch?

By the time I got to high school, I still shrank from the notion of the impure, but feelings and attractions and explorations had entered my adolescent life. The nuns knew this, of course—they were no dummies—and our instructions got more specific.

I learned what a French kiss was and that it was impure. A kiss that was not a French kiss but went on too long was impure. Sitting on a boy's lap was impure. Trying to "lead a boy on"—what did that mean, exactly?—was impure. Most of us had some semblance of breasts: letting a boy touch our breasts was impure. Sister actually said "breasts" to us.

We sat silent in our desks.

Gregorian Chant and the Congo

On Friday nights we had choir practice. Gregorian chant loomed hugely in our lives. The proper pitch. The proper breath control. The proper reading of the notes. Breathing from the diaphragm. Getting up above the note mentally in order to hit it properly when we sang it out. Proper posture. The proper pronunciation of the Latin. Not *gloria in ex-cel-sis*—not that, not *cel* as "sell"—but *gloria in egg-shell-sis* was the proper way to say it.

Sister S., the choir director, was a woman of stature in the

Gregorian chant network. She had authored a book on chant. She had a wooden clicker, which always struck me as a kind of castanet, that marked the beats—the quarter notes, the half notes, and the rests. She also sometimes clicked it rapidly to signal us to stop what we were singing, that the way we were singing was just too awful: *"No, no, no, Sisters."*

She marched up and down the aisles of the chapel, hearing the music from behind, hearing it from the front; and up to the choir loft, hearing us from above, listening to the schola's responsories, listening to the organ. She was a woman who was determined that music and singing be performed as perfectly as possible for the Lord, for one another, and for the continuance of the tradition of Gregorian chant.

Her head was always cocked; she was listening. Too bad that a veil fell over her ears, because even that thinnest of black fabrics must have kept her from hearing as she preferred to hear music.

Sister S. was immersed in her work to the degree that it must have been like Sister Luke in the Congo, where the latter enjoyed medicine so much that it meant a kind of inner freedom from the demands and strictures of the community. Gregorian chant was Sister Mary S.'s Congo.

She loved music so much that she barely noticed where she was. Perfection of the life had been taken care of by being a nun. It freed her to concentrate on that other perfection: perfection of the work.

Treats

We had treats daily, usually in the afternoon during a brief period of recreation; they were served on small greenish plates and each

Sister could pick one up from the novitiate table. The plates had mostly candy on them. A piece of chocolate or two, some hard candy, maybe some jelly beans. But it was all sugar.

Outside of treat time, we didn't eat. It was never all right to go to cupboards or dresser drawers when we were hungry and simply help ourselves to something. Never. We did have adequate meals, but there were no snacks besides the one treat plate. All edible goods in packages sent by our families were donated to the common treat supply cupboard.

By midafternoon in the convent I was always hungry. When I came into the novitiate, I eyed the plates that had been set up and filled by others as part of their duty. Most of us were glad we didn't have treat duty; it would have been like a practicing alcoholic inheriting a bar. We all knew by then that we should not look for the best or the fullest treat plate, that a person should just take the one closest to her when she came in the door or approached the table.

Some days I did as I was supposed to do. On other days I circled the table, sizing up the plates, looking for the fullest one or for one that had the most pieces of chocolate. And when I had polished off the candy, I felt as if I could have bitten the plate, too, and chewed the green plastic chunks right up for whatever invisible gumdrop fragments and milk chocolate fragrance were left on it.

On some days my need—for *what?*—was great.

I felt angry and guilty for feeling angry when our Novice Mistress told us what one of the professed Sisters in the motherhouse had said about her own need to eat. The heat had gone out one time in the winter and this Sister said she had to keep eating to stay warm. I took it that she could indeed eat outside of regular meal times, and I was angry because I wanted to do that, too.

I did not enjoy such a privilege and I felt like a child or a speck. The Novice Mistress had chuckled with sympathy as she told this story but I did not think it was one bit funny. That Sister had what sounded like a measure of freedom, maybe the considerations that an officer might have in the military, and I was the enlisted person. Of course. The novitiate was the boot camp of the religious life.

I did hear stories. Some of my own peers from time to time brazenly violated the rule that read, "Without permission no one shall eat out of the accustomed time and place." Some regularly hid apples in the pockets of their ample black serge skirts. And one of us, one angelic-looking one, somehow had two laundry bags: she had set up one for dirty clothes and another for candy. We did have unannounced inspection of our dormitory alcoves, but what Novice Mistress would look in a laundry bag? Had the culprit raided the treat cupboard? Was she receiving packages from home, the contents of which went right into the laundry bag? How had she gotten up the nerve to do this?

And why had God not made *me* more brazen in spite of myself?

Birds and French

On February 2, 1962, my set became the senior novices. And we watched the new group of postulants become junior novices. We felt important, being careful that this not lead to pride.

So, back to secular studies. The names of the classes we took sounded so worldly. French. Library science.

Most of us adored the Sister who taught library science. Sister E. wasn't the kind of nun on whom anyone would get a crush. We just plain loved her. Her skin was swarthy and she had the finest sense of humor. She also was a birdwatcher, which struck me as slightly off—for a nun. The Dewey Decimal System was often punctuated with stories of birds she had seen. Once, while watching an owl, she had been bitten by a bat and she had to have the dreaded series of rabies shots. Birdwatching was her Congo. Owls were her Congo.

Hope sat on my shoulder like a parakeet when I was in her class. If someone like this nun existed, things would be all right; she reminded me of some of the high school teachers I'd had. She was not spooky and cavernous and basically chilly like the Novice Mistresses. She was a little plump and happy and tolerant and funny and unsentimental and she had her birds. Perhaps I would be lucky enough, in the end, to be assigned to the convent where this woman resided.

It struck me as funny that we novices were also taking French, which I had started studying when I was at Clarke. But people in nuns' habits speaking French? If we had lived in France as nuns, we would naturally enough be speaking French, but saying things like *"J'ai faim"* and *"J'ai soif"* when we no longer uttered these things in our native English struck me as incongruous. Those phrases were strongly about needs, and we were trying to be basically needless, detached.

"Ma soeur," which Sister R., a fine teacher, said over and over again to us, also sounded odd to me. *"Ma."* It was possessive. It was idiomatically correct. "My sister." I balked internally when I used the phrase. Was it because I had been involved studying canon law and natural theology and the follies of Renan and Bultmann for a whole year? Now to be asking, *"Avez-vous un stylo, ma soeur?"* seemed a little silly.

And didn't affection lurk somewhere behind the phrase? The possessive implies a relationship and I was bent on not developing one of those connections with anybody.

And then—French became for me, in an instant, luminous.

We used a small language lab in the motherhouse in connection with our studies. I found a recording of some kind of French opera or operetta to do with Joan of Arc. I had not paid attention when I was young, but sitting in the language lab, I was struck with the thought that *Joan spoke French.*

There was nothing pretentious about *Jeanne d'Arc,* about any French words used to describe her. I listened to the recording over and over again. Joan is *"fille de Dieu."* In this French, Joan not only heard the saints' voices. They actually sang to her: *"Fille de Dieu, fille de Dieu: Va, va, va."*

And I remembered that I was part French, too.

The Train Whistle

Doubts seized me during the summer when I was a senior novice. Should I really be a nun? Maybe I should go home and resume my life in the world. Like Tessa. For she had left.

The doubts made me cringe. From where in the world had they come?

I could find no explanation for what gripped me. The doubts seemed simply to have arisen, like a genie out of a lamp or a bottle. Or they popped up like a balloon with words in it, words being spoken by a character in a comic strip in the *St. Paul Pioneer Press:* Prince Valiant? Dick Tracy? The Katzenjammer Kids?

The genie followed me everywhere in his oversized, tear-shaped cloud. The comic strip balloon with the indecipherable print in it trailed along behind me as if it were tied to my wrist, from the chapel to the kitchen to the Pine Walk. I came to fear and loathe the genie and the balloon doubts. I even had them when or just after I received communion.

The train I had ridden to Dubuque on July 31, 1960, was clearly visible across the water, across the Mississippi, from the high ground on which Mount Carmel stood. I sometimes paused on the front lawn outside the convent and saw that small, long, silver train with several cars. Its whistle became a torture to me.

It occurred to me that my doubts about whether I should really be a nun were coming from a delayed reaction: severe homesickness was what it was. I was homesick for home and for the world, the world Tessa was now enjoying.

And the train would take me back to that world. Get on at Dubuque and then ride north to Prairie du Chien, Winona, and finally Saint Paul.

I did not focus on what I would do when I got home; I focused on what my train experience would be, should I leave. I imagined myself in my old lay clothing stepping onto the train. And once on, there would be a conductor—I would love to see a fatherly, knowledgeable conductor again.

I would settle into a seat, and hear "All aboard," with "board" receiving a rising intonation at the end. Once I was on, the train would start to move, slowly at first, and then, as it picked up speed, the rocking or swaying motion would set in. I would be by myself for the first time in two years.

I would not need to think about the rule all the time. There would be decisions to be made. I would have the luxury of going to the dome car without asking anyone, without consulting a soul. It would be warm and sunny up there and spacious, and I could watch the Iowa countryside pass by. There were bathrooms, albeit jiggly ones.

Some one of the nuns would surely have given me a little money when I left—my *dowry,* of *course*—or asked my parents for some for me, so I would go to the dining car at noon. I loved that moving room of pure white tablecloths and napkins, heavy silver, vases of flowers, interesting menus, good smells, and white-coated waiters who would care for my needs. How much fun to eat and at the same time be going somewhere. And if I agreed, someone else might sit at my table.

All possible imagery surrounding the train was compressed in its prolonged and meditative whistle. It made me flinch.

At that time I was in a dorm on the very top floor of the convent. It held more than the usual dorm room—more flapping white curtains, more beds, more dressers. The windows were open because of the intense heat, the humid air. And the train whistle carried and crossed the river and crossed the room and came to me in my bed.

The whistle was a god. Bent on doing what?

I had to do something about it. This being torn, I thought, is malignant.

I had had thoughts. Doubts. Well, I would banish them. The genie, I convinced myself, was the devil. The Katzenjammer Kids were little devils. Dick Tracy's antagonist was Satan. I had to fight with Prince Valiant against the Huns, those Beelzebubs, with my magic Singing Sword whose name was Flamberge.

Perhaps I had suffered the three temptations of Christ when He was out in the desert. The genie offered me the kingdoms of this world; the Katzenjammer Kids wanted me to challenge der Captain, Mama, and der Inspector and then go jump off a cliff; Dick Tracy's opponent wanted to take me to a diner for French toast, for which I was very hungry.

And the old, oft-rehearsed logic followed: if I had a calling, a vocation to religious life, I needed to follow it. I could refuse a vocation, but who in her right mind would do that? Say no to what the Supreme Being was calling you to do? Who would do that?

But this time I added a twist: I conjured up a further insight. Since I was so acutely *aware* that being a nun was the perfect way to serve God, that in itself *marked* me. That must mean that I actually had a vocation.

So I would stay.

I felt quite peaceful again. The peace of a firm decision.

What train whistle? What lush dining car? I ignored all of it.

My path was secure. I was secure. The poor rest of those souls out in the world, battered about, unsure of themselves, living a secular life, had chosen second best. I had been chosen and I had, once again, chosen the more perfect way.

I stuffed the genie back into his lamp. I shut the newspaper comics section so quickly and so hard that the paper made a rattling, snapping sound.

Skin

But my skin was not cooperating with my newfound peace. I began to suffer from acne, with which I had not been especially bothered in high school.

Now lesions appeared that were deep and painful: cystic acne. It was humiliating. Sister Luke had not had acne. No nuns that I could think of had serious acne—maybe a small pimple once in a while on one of my nun-teachers' faces (and even that embarrassed me), but that was all.

Was this some kind of imperfection in me? Were my emotions acting up? This was a blight that seemed incongruous now that I had renewed my decision to be a nun, now that peace had come to me.

I began to think of it as some kind of poison in my system. I did not think much about the fact that my brother had also had cystic acne and that it had dragged on for years, treatment being a rarity when he was in high school.

I waited for it to wear itself out. And I waited. And it did not wear itself out. What kind of a nun would a nun with acne be?

And after the once-a-year day when families were allowed to visit for a few hours, my Novice Mistress approached me. "Sister, your mother thought perhaps you should go to the doctor for your skin."

What? My mother had said nothing of this to me.

"To the dermatologist, Sister." My parents would pay for it. For years now they had been comfortable financially.

I had to wear a black veil to go "out." I had to change so that people would not think I was a novice. Novices did not go out.

I was a fraud but the black veil looked wonderful, I thought. And for one day every three weeks I had a cab ride to a doctor in Dubuque, who decided that the treatment of choice was the UV lamp. And for a day or two after that, at recreation, my fellow novices would say, "Sister, your face is so *red!*" I was not supposed to tell them that I had gone out for these treatments.

The mystery was why an apparent exception had been made for me for such a condition. Perhaps that's why parental visits were limited. Too much interference. Too much meddling. Too many requests that were logical. Too much that was hard for a superior to turn down in a weak moment.

The one and only thing my superior ever said to me about this was (after I was released by the doctor from the visits to the sunshine of the summer months), "Sister, your skin looks so much better." I don't think anyone had said *anything* to me about a specific part of my body for the years that I was in the convent. My skin: it looked better.

Acne I knew I had. But skin? Did I have skin?

Like Chocolate

For several days we were to read from a book we had been given in preparation for Instructions. The subject was sex.

What did I know of sex coming into the convent?

My mother had suddenly one day handed me a book, when I was about fourteen or fifteen. It was a small book with a dark leather cover and it explained not only sex but also the rhythm method, which sounded very spooky, very scary.

I remembered a section about the man and the woman having to be very close to each other in bed, facing each other. But the book was not very detailed beyond this.

We had guppies in the family aquarium and I was a big guppy-watcher. There were often pregnant guppies, gravid, dark in their bellies: this led to baby guppies, which had to be fished out quickly so they wouldn't be eaten. But there were also male guppies, and I studied them and the little appendages that occasionally bent out into the water for a time.

After much reflection, I had thought that if I wanted to have a child, which in itself was unlikely, I would circumvent all this murk and embarrassment and untidy-sounding activity and adopt. Orphans were out there who needed to be adopted anyway.

The book we read in the novitiate explained the hydraulics of sex. The explicit part, the paragraph that contained the words "penis" and "penetration" and "vagina," came on the right-hand side of a page about two-fifths of the way down. So now I knew. Now I could be sure that I knew what happened.

Some young women knew a lot more than I did much earlier. Obviously: one of my acquaintances—at Our Lady of Peace!— actually got pregnant and dropped out of school, an event that set all of us reeling. I tried to imagine how Kitty and her boyfriend could have accomplished this, but I had trouble. Maybe it had started with Daniel touching her breasts, which did, I had noticed, stand way out. With most of us, the boys probably wondered just where our breasts were located, exactly, under our blouses.

Kitty and Daniel—how had they gotten the privacy? I stopped there. To actively imagine more would have gotten me into the impure zone. Sin. But I had used my imagination in putting the sinister rhythm method book and my guppy watching together. The man and the woman had to lie very close to each other (as in the book) because the man's appendage, which would stick out, had to get inside the woman (the guppy part).

"Sisters," the Novice Mistress said, "listen. You *need* to know what you are giving up when you take the vow of chastity." The novitiate seemed even more austere and solemn and quiet that day.

"They say," she said, "that sexual intercourse is very pleasurable." (Instantly I knew! Sister herself had never had sexual intercourse.) "So be aware that you are giving up something that can be gratifying.

"But it is quite indescribable, I imagine," she said. "So it would be hard to understand the particulars of the gratification."

Just as, she told us, it would be hard to comprehend what chocolate was like if you had never eaten chocolate.

Well, sexual intercourse must be good, then. I loved chocolate.

But I sensed something about her analogy. Eating chocolate was finally such a solitary occupation. And that romantic, thrilling part of sex that I had experienced and loved, the kissing, involved someone else. A boy. Boys.

Boys. Boys who were slightly foreign but fetching in their maleness. Young men who were subtle and curious and who wore plaid shirts that smelled different from my blouses. Boys who could be funny and who were smart in chemistry class and who wore Canoe by Dana (classified as a "refined" men's fragrance) on dates.

Did all that go away in sex?

. . .

Did you sort of end up forgetting the boy was there so that you felt like you were by yourself with a sweet lump of chocolate in your mouth? That would be a little too bad.

Something of a Nuisance

I do remember, though, that the sex instruction in the convent was followed with a caveat about sex not being what it was cracked up to be.

It went like this: our Novice Mistress and another nun had been talking with a married, wealthy laywoman whom they knew well. This woman said that she didn't much enjoy sex and that it was something of a nuisance.

Oh. I think we were shocked that our Novice Mistress would be talking about sex with a laywoman but we were impressed by the conversation. I was sitting at the middle table in the novitiate when she spoke these words. "Something of a nuisance." Maybe so.

If this was true, then taking a vow of chastity didn't seem bad at all. I would never know what it was like and whether it was pleasurable or a nuisance or pleasurable *and* a nuisance, and in the latter case which outweighed which, but that was all right.

I hadn't climbed mountains either. I *had* tasted chocolate. I had even tasted pheasant (ring-necked), although it hadn't been served under glass. And I had never had ortolan, with a giant linen napkin draped over my head while I crunched it, bones and all. I had had a Manhattan in Manhattan. I had smoked. I had never ridden an elephant. I had had confused and complicated exchanges with young men who seemed unaccountably fervent and urgent at times and distant and arrogant at other times. There were lots of things I hadn't done.

I couldn't do everything. Not having sex would be OK. It was all pretty abstract. It would be fine.

And of course I would be "giving up" babies along with that. My memories of babies were fading: they had seemed cute but if they cried for a long time when I was babysitting, I grew bored with them and impatient and wished the parents would come back from their cocktail parties or dinners so I could go home.

Tumor

Sometime during my year as a senior novice, word came that my mother had a brain tumor. The Novice Mistress called me in to tell me that my sister had called. A neurosurgeon would operate on the brain tumor.

A brain tumor was something spectacular, something I could not imagine. It sounded like something out of the annals of the history of science. I was totally disoriented and didn't know how I was supposed to respond. People usually asked about a patient's chances in such a situation and I thought to do that.

"Fifty-fifty, Sister. A fifty-fifty chance of cure."

Somehow or other, my superior decided that I should not go home then; that I could go home sometime in the future after my mother had recuperated a bit. I accepted this.

Brain cancer was terrible, frightening. That my mother, whom I loved, had it was terrible.

How could I respond?

There was nothing to do but pray and write to her.

My sister and my brother were both married and had children so they couldn't physically move into our old house and help my father take care of my mother.

But I was in a way also married, I said to myself. And Christ came first.

Even so, I did begin to wonder a little about how decided my superior had been about my not going home "just now." Did she have an ulterior motive? Was she concerned that I would get back to Saint Paul and get caught up amid various blandishments and fall under the spell of the old world?

She needn't have worried. She could have counted on how well I had learned that a call to the religious life came before everything.

Her Power

There was a certain type of nun in a position of leadership in those days at the motherhouse whom I admired and who also frightened me. This type was sophisticated, had lived in a large city in her girlhood. This nun was bright, highly literate. This nun carried herself well, with a certain amount of ease admixed with the fine posture of the aligned marbles.

This nun had expressive eyes and wore her habit with grace. Gestures of hers were definite. She was savvy about internal affairs at the highest level of the community. She had a sense of humor; she was sharp. She had some power.

But there was something—something. A steeliness underneath the occasional displays of warmth. The watchfulness, always threatening to turn into disapproval, of an administrator who lacked greatness. And a hint of fragility and a whiff of— what was it—nostalgia? Unhappiness?

Nuns of this type seemed to me to be highly ambitious; somehow the convent that had in the name of God nurtured this had at the same time foiled it. An aura of sadness, an aura of rue walked where these nuns walked. Whether they admitted these feelings to themselves or not, they turned to expending their energy on "forming" us, the young ones.

I caught myself meditating on this subject with some surprise and with some guilt.

These were my Sisters; some of them were my superiors, crucial links in the great Chain of Being. And here I was analyzing them as if they were merely human.

Drama

There was in our set a talented woman, now Sister N., who had come in with a degree in drama. When we were senior novices she had the idea that we should put on a play. A play? Our superiors must have conferred: Sister N. was given permission. We would put on the play in our habits.

How would this work? Nuns dashing about playing the roles of people who weren't nuns? It seemed ludicrous. But daring.

What play would be selected? It turned out to be *The Diary of Anne Frank*, adapted for the stage by Frances Goodrich and Albert Hackett and first performed at the Cort Theatre, New York City, in October 1955.

Anne Frank had hidden from the Gestapo with seven other Jews in a small attic above a warehouse in Amsterdam. The little group lived under these impossibly constricted circumstances for two years and one month, until they were discovered.

I had read and reread the English translation of the diary itself in the mid-1950s, when I was in early adolescence—as Anne had been when she wrote her diary. Pretending I was Anne in her attic, I would look out my bedroom window at bits of sky.

Anne had died in the Nazi concentration camp at Bergen-Belsen in March 1945. But I was still alive, going about convent living in America. Everyone, including our superiors, was enthusiastic about our project and that we were working with this particular story. We, dressed as nuns, were proudly going to put on the play about a Jew in Amsterdam. Anne was our heroine.

I was eventually cast as the mother, Mrs. Frank. I was always cast as the mother.

Why?

I was cast as the mother in my high school's production of *The Song of Bernadette* and as the mother in *Mother Was a Freshman* in high school. I was somebody's black-wigged mother in an adaptation of *The Little World of Don Camillo* put on at Saint Thomas Academy. Here I was, the one who had dismissed the idea of being a mother, a mother again.

We were excused from evening recreations to go to the infirmary, which had a somewhat large auditorium downstairs, to rehearse. What were the superiors thinking? Though we had not been specifically told this, I thought the ideal in all things was not to *stand out*. No particular friendships. No singularities. Habits or nunly uniforms would distinguish us out in the world but not among ourselves. Nothing eccentric or idiomatic.

Now we were surely singled out. We were the chosen. It felt good to be special in this way, in any way.

No doubt a bond grew between us. This was fertile ground for friendships. We didn't spend a lot of time talking about ourselves to one another during the time when we rehearsed, but we grew closer together as a cast.

Learning my lines was easier than it had been for high school plays. Learning anything was easier. If we were trained to do anything, we were trained to read and study as well as to meditate. No distractions.

Sister N. was a born director with a difference. She had a good sense of design; she was self-confident. She was not temperamental. She was smart, funny, precise in her movements. She had expressive eyebrows. She was more mature than the rest of us.

We put on the play for the whole community with minimal props and dressed in our habits (minus leather belts, and the long dangling rosaries with their crucifixes).

The Blessed Virgin Cries

The clouds of glory I trailed when I was born included, I was convinced, being expressive. But I did not grow up to be actively expressive. Everything inveighed against that. The Church. Sin. Worry over my parents.

Try being expressive when mortal sin lurked right around the corner of your deeds, right at the edge of every envelope, right on the rim of the plate that held too much food, right below the border of the plaid cummerbund that your boyfriend wore with his tux to the prom. Or try it when someone said or quoted someone who had said, "Every time a little girl whistles, the Blessed Virgin cries." And try it if you do not have a disposition where you can easily say "Nuts" or say nothing and do as you please.

But on the stage you could do anything. You could be really expressive. "She" was not you. It was perfect. On the stage you could raise your voice. You could run around on the set, which was a more controllable world than the real one.

My childhood home, on its large corner lot, come to think of it, had multiple stages and experimental theaters, labs, hospitals, and circuses, inside and out. Every fall I was the master architect for the spacious leaf houses I used to rake into floor-plan shapes in Saint Paul. I was a physician with my little doctor's kit.

The best of all was being able to operate on the miniature, the small world. My dollhouse had me for director, producer, and playwright. My brother's collection of balsa model airplanes and ships astonished me every time I was allowed into his room.

To make a faux map of Treasure Island for your model pirates' ship, pencil-sketch it on dove-colored parchment paper which is 1½ inches by 2 inches. When you are satisfied, darken the lines in black ink. You may color the sea a deep blue.

You can feather the edges of the map by using gold paint. You can use a trimmed bamboo skewer to roll up the edges of the map as desired so that it will look scroll-like on the miniature brown charting desk that you had earlier buffed to a glossy finish. Position the map at a slant on the desk.

You could build and arrange, decorate and move things. You could construct dialogues and be passionate and not hurt anyone. What your characters said and did would be their sins, theirs to confess, not yours. You could let down your guard. You could quit, even if for a short time, being so watchful.

The Scream

I grew to love my part in the play. A Jewish mother. Anne Frank's mother. A great part. Mrs. Frank is constantly worried, of course. She's crabby at times. Hysterical at times.

After all the practicing, opening night arrived. Almost the whole community of nuns was assembled. I concentrated, I tried to project myself as Mrs. Frank might have done. She was especially passionate and angry when Mr. Van Daan stole some of the group's bread at night. That bread had been strictly rationed.

Sister N. had *not* said I should tone it down.

We tried, not very successfully, for some kind of accent.

"Da *bread!*" I cried. Mr. Van Daan had reached into the food safe in the middle of the night and had drawn out the end of a loaf of bread, but I had heard the safe door creak. I had seen him.

(All of MRS. FRANK's *gentleness, her self-control is gone. She is outraged, in a frenzy of indignation.)*

MRS. FRANK

The bread! He was stealing the bread!

As Mrs. Frank, I decided I would kick the Van Daans out of the attic, out of hiding. I told them to take their things and get out. Let the Nazis get them. My pitch rose. My husband, Otto Frank, became alarmed.

MR. FRANK

(*To* MRS. FRANK)

You're speaking in anger. You cannot mean what you are saying.

MRS. FRANK

I mean exactly that!

Otto became more alarmed. He was thunderstruck at how adamant I was.

MR. FRANK

Edith, I've never seen you like this before. I don't know you.

MRS. FRANK

I should have spoken out long ago.

The miracle of it was that by all reports our little cast made the audience forget that the actresses were dressed in nuns' habits. We ourselves had completely forgotten about it some time earlier. It was strange. I thought for days about how the habits had vanished by virtue of the power of the imagination.

After the closing scenes, when the Germans discover the Frank family; after the recording, procured somehow by Sister N., of the Gestapo sirens; after the set completely darkened, the play ended.

There was silence in the large audience of nuns. Then they applauded. They passed congratulations all around.

The next day, Sister Y. seemed not too pleased and spoke in Instructions of some overacting on our parts. I thought of myself as one of the most emotional, most expressive characters in the play, so Sister Y. must have had me in mind. I had to be the one to whom she was referring.

She may have been right. I was not sure. Shame lay on me for a few days.

But still, telling someone to get out had felt somewhat right.

Get out. . . . I mean exactly that! . . . I should have spoken out long ago. What bold, assertive things to say.

I knew about Stanislavsky's method acting from my high school drama class. I had not been able to withdraw to an attic for weeks to experience what the Frank family had experienced but I had reached down and drawn on my resources. How, I wondered, had I been able to find in myself a "frenzy of indignation"? Feelings of indignation were foreign to me, weren't they?

And screaming. I had screamed, and it was so out-and-out like—*something*. Like something *what*? Like something *good*?

A Snap

February 1963 was approaching. February 2 was approaching, the day when my set would make our first temporary vows.

I felt I knew exactly what I was doing. I had studied and meditated and examined myself. I was ready. The vows were evangelical counsels, based somewhere or other in scripture. They were not for everyone. But this way was the shortest route to perfection.

I knew that by vowing poverty, for example, I would be giving up ownership of everything. All that I had, I would use but not possess. This vow led right back to the story of Jesus' encounter with the young man who wanted to be perfect but couldn't give up, in the end, all his material goods.

But I would not turn away sad, like that young man. I would do it. I would give up everything, own nothing, work for the community for nothing, follow Christ. It would be a snap.

True, from the time I was a preteen when my parents had some money again, I had liked things and especially clothes— cinch belts, crinolines, saddle shoes, peasant blouses, felt skirts, spike heels, shirtwaist dresses. To shuck all of that did not seem much of a problem. I was going for something higher. Besides. I had the beautiful classic black and the sharply contrasting white to wear.

Poverty pointed in a positive direction. It meant spirituality and a sort of freedom and the development of the life of the mind in a way that I didn't think laywomen with all sorts of trappings could manage. It meant simplification. We had studied it in the Constitutions.

THE VOW AND THE VIRTUE OF POVERTY

77. By the simple vow of Poverty the Sisters renounce the right of licitly disposing of or using any temporal thing whatsoever of monetary value without permission of their lawful Superiors.

78. The Sisters are forbidden to retain personally the administration of any of their property.

88. The Sisters cannot ascribe or reserve to themselves whatever they may acquire by their own industry or in behalf of the Congregation after they have made their vows. All these things must be regarded as the property of the Community for the common advantage of the Congregation or the house.

89. All things in the Congregation, as furnishings, food, and clothing, shall be considered, and shall be, common. It is fitting, however, that those garments which are for strictly personal use, although regarded as common, should be kept and distributed separately.

90. The furnishings which the Sisters use, with permission of their Superiors, should be consistent with Poverty; there should be nothing superfluous, yet nothing necessary should be refused.

91. All who desire to live in this Congregation should with great love cherish Holy Poverty, which Jesus

Christ our Lord and His Blessed Mother so diligently practiced; let them be content, therefore, with things merely necessary, according to the spirit and customs of the Community.

92. That this may more easily prevail, no Sister shall hold anything as her own, but all things shall be possessed in common. Hence, no one is allowed to have anything or to use anything as her own, to lend or accept or give anything belonging to the house, without the consent of the Superior.

93. Should they perceive that they need anything, let them with great simplicity make it known to the Sister whose duty it is to provide for all in the Lord.

94. The Sister to whom the office of providing is assigned shall carefully ascertain what is necessary for the Sisters and shall supply this with great charity, observing both the spirit of Poverty and the means of the Community.

95. In regard to clothing and all other things which the Sisters can use, they should not put aside nor alter anything without the special consent of the Superior.

96. They should use most discreetly any money committed to their care and should understand that they sin against the vow of Poverty whenever they use even the smallest amount without the permission of the Superior, at least reasonably presumed.

97. That the Poverty which befits our Congregation may be most carefully observed, no one, not even the Superior General, shall be allowed to depart in any way from the simplicity and the spirit of our Poverty, as regards clothing, food, and furnishings.

In the practical keeping of the vow of poverty, everything was aimed at the good of the community. If someone gave you a gift, you either refused it or gave it to your superior. If you inherited money, it went to the community. You did not, at that time, accept gifts that had strings attached, that stipulated, for example, that the money had to be used for your benefit in such and such a way.

What would we have done with money anyway? We had everything we needed. We had clothing, three meals a day, plus treats in the afternoon; a clean residence that was kept in good repair. Who looked at the roof, who maintained the walkways and the grounds? The Boys, not us.

We would receive a college education from our order. Free. We would end up with bachelor's degrees and some of us would obtain master's degrees and doctorates. Free. The community had elementary schools and secondary schools all over the country and it had two colleges.

The community had a future. Vocations, the numbers of people who felt themselves called by God to enter religious life, were both for the BVMs and for other orders in the United States at an all-time high.

So we had futures and those futures went straight on toward death, and death itself meant only a more intense future. If in the meantime we became ill or grew old and infirm, we would be lovingly taken care of by other Sisters in the community's equivalent of a nursing home: Marian Hall, on the Mount Carmel grounds.

We would be buried in our own private cemetery, the one to which we walked every morning on the Pine Walk. We would have a headstone with our name in religion and with the date of our birth on it. Most of us would reach old age and many of us would reach the age called the "oldest old"—eighties, late eighties, nineties.

On a more immediate level, there was a supply closet for shampoo, deodorant, and the like from which I could help myself. It was not all a single brand—there were usually a couple of choices. Pads of paper were there for note taking; pencils and pens were there.

Who paid all the bills for these things and for electricity, for clothes that had to be replaced as they wore out, for groceries? Not us.

I would never see a bill unless I became a superior. I would never see a balance sheet. I would never see a checkbook. I would probably never know how the community was doing financially. Never again would I worry about whether or not I had money, whether I could afford to go to the dentist or to the doctor.

A Watch Face

Late in the period of the novitiate, I did receive one thing that was hard not to think of as mine—a wristwatch. As the day of profession of vows loomed, we had all been given permission to let our parents know that they could present us with watches.

During our instruction period one day, the watch was the subject of discussion. The watch should be fairly plain.

"And, Sisters, the watch face should not be too big."

My watch arrived in the mail: my parents had gone to the jeweler's together to pick it out. The jeweler's.

I imagined the inside of a jewelry store and my mother—whose hair had grown back out by now—and father, with diamonds and rubies and pearl chokers all around them, looking at watches.

The watch was an Omega and it was lovely in its simplicity. But the face, the face of it was a little large; it bordered on being too large, I thought.

Oh no, I thought. Would I be able to wear it?

When the members of my set received their watches they were to present them to the Novice Mistress for inspection and approval. I was almost sure I knew what would happen as I approached Sister Y. Too large.

She looked at my Omega. "That's all right, Sister," she said to me.

All right?

Had she looked at it closely enough?

I now had my own watch, but it was not my own. It was mine to use in this world.

My parents had good taste but I reminded myself not to be too proud about it or too proud of this Omega watch. And I nudged myself so that I would stop imagining all the sparkling going on inside a fine Saint Paul jewelry store.

The watch made me happy, strapped just above my wrist.

Wrist Bones

The Omega watch reminded me for a moment that I had an actual wrist. I had studied about wrist bones.

ॐ

Eight carpal bones make up the wrist: navicular, lunate, triquetrum, pisiform, trapezium, trapezoid, capitate, hamate.

ॐ

But bones didn't matter much. And I dismissed the fact that not only did I have wrist bones but they were uniquely mine.

Bones were secular, weren't they? Part of the mortal coil to be shuffled off.

Another Snap

I just knew I would do well practicing the vow of obedience. I had studied the rule months earlier. It would be, like poverty, another snap. Again, I understood exactly what was expected of me. Explanations of things theological could get quite elaborate, like all the logical Aquinian proofs for the existence of God, but the day-to-day living of Holy Obedience was pretty simple.

Simple in the extreme as a matter of fact: your Sister superior's will for you is expressive of the Will of God. If the superior has you on the duty list for scrubbing toilets, that is God's Will for you. How positively joyful that you are certain that when you are cleaning the toilets, that is God's Will.

If the superior's superior, the Mother General of the order, sends you to Memphis to teach, that is God's Will for you. If a cardinal under the authority of the Pope issues an instruction through the Sacred Congregation for Religious and your superiors incorporate it into the policies of your community, then that, again, is God's Will for you. This was not the same thing as the infallibility of the Pope—limited only to matters of faith and doctrine—but still, it was a lockstep chain, a mediation of God's Will.

I had been trying to practice versions of this throughout my life. "Honor thy father and mother" meant, we were taught in school, to be obedient to parents. Besides, they were the people who had brought you into the world and they were the peo-

ple who took care of you. I broke the commandment, though: I
had gotten angry with my parents sometimes and it had become
matter for confession.

But especially now that I was going to become a nun, I
wouldn't have a problem. Nuns did not break the Holy Rule or go
against their vows. For *sure* they didn't break any command-
ments. The thought of a nun breaking a *commandment* struck me
as funny.

Obedience would be a snap.

It had been hard for Sister Luke, but that part of *The Nun's
Story* had baffled me. I did have a passing thought that her problem may have arisen because she was older, already a nurse when
she entered. Maybe set in her ways? The way I had heard old
bachelors became.

The lines of authority were clear. They ran all the way back
to the Pope and to God and it just took all the uncertainty out of
things.

Maybe Sister Luke just didn't get it.

The way I did.

His Hem

As for chastity, on February 2 I was more than ready. I was
presently practicing chastity, was I not? The Novice Mistress had
made sure we understood what happened in the act of sex. What
was there to give up, really? I couldn't see how it would pinch
much. The Constitutions handed us the details.

98. By the Vow of Chastity a Sister, in making Profession, binds herself to the observance of celibacy; and
moreover, by a new title, that is, the virtue of religion, to

abstain from every act whatsoever, either internal or external, opposed to Chastity.

99. In regard to this holy virtue let the Sisters understand how earnestly they must strive to cultivate angelic purity with all zeal; hence they should most diligently avoid everything contrary to the spirit of this virtue; for instance, the desire of seeing and hearing everything, long conversations with seculars, and the wish to attract the attention of others whether interns or externs.

100. This they will more easily observe if such modesty of the eyes and of the whole person be apparent in them that they may be an example to all and may never become subject to even the slightest suspicion of anything contrary to the angelic virtue.

101. To preserve this virtue properly, let them be convinced that although exterior mortification is a great help thereunto, yet unless this be accompanied by interior mortification, by which the intellect and the will and all desires of flesh and blood are kept in subjection under the guidance of obedience, it will neither last long nor profit much. Moreover great help will be derived from frequent reception of Holy Communion, the practice of humility and devotion to the Blessed Virgin Mary.

And what I would get in return! I would be a bride of Christ. No mediation through a human being. I would be directly wed to Christ, even though my superiors wisely downplayed such imagery and spoke instead of consecrated virginity. I would be His (He must be male because He was male on earth).

I couldn't see Him, true. But wait. There was something, Somebody there. A Presence. And I could, this side of the grave, see Him in others, serve Him in others.

When I died I would see Him. I would, as Saint Paul described it, be caught up into the air—not just join Him in the air but be "caught up" into the air—with Him, and that would be something beyond measure. The Church was His bride and I would be His bride.

How could a mere man compete with that? For sure, none of the boys I had gone out with could.

But it was nice that He was a Man because I had basically liked men. Men were different from me and that was interesting.

How did the men religious think of Him? As Christ the brother?

I couldn't touch Him, but I could imagine doing so. I had often imagined touching His hem as the woman with the bloody issue had done in scripture. That woman had been healed.

I imagined His hem as whitish, the fabric coarse. When I placed my index finger lightly on that fabric, He felt it and asked, "Who touched me?" Then He turned around.

And in my imagination, after His crucifixion, like Magdalene, I tried to touch Him again. I encountered Him in the garden near His own tomb, although at first I mistook Him for the old gardener because He looked terrible. But this time He warned me not to touch Him because He had not as yet ascended to His Father, which made so little sense to me that I felt like arguing.

I was Mary Magdalene in all senses save that of a history of adultery.

PART THREE

Making Vows

Vow Day

February 2, the feast of the Purification, was Vow Day.

One by one during the service of profession, in the context of the Mass, we rose from our pews and said as distinctly as possible: "I, Sister Mary ———, vow to Thee poverty, chastity, and obedience for one year."

Then we processed out and, with the assistance of others, unpinned the white veils and pinned on the black veils. When we appeared back in the chapel we were professed Sisters of Charity of the Blessed Virgin Mary.

My Dominican aunt, Sister Mary Cleopha, was in the chapel that day. My parents, my family, laypeople in general were not invited. But any relative in religious life, priest or nun, received an invitation. "Aunt Sis," as we children always called her, had been slightly chagrined that I did not choose to enter her own Dominican order but she handled it all with grace.

My mother had for a time taught Latin at the Racine high school where Aunt Sis was teaching: Mother provided constant conversation for the nuns. She, Connie, was their doll.

I think my lively mother verged on the scandalous for the nuns in the Dominican convent and that they lived a bit vicariously through her. She had that curly hair and wore red dresses and was working on a master's degree at Marquette.

They tried to convince my mother that she should be a nun.

"One day," Mother told me, "they even dressed me up like a nun. But," she went on, "I escaped. I 'leaped over the wall.' "

There was a tale about her not liking it that the lamps in the convent parlor had fringes on the lamp shades. She thought that looked ungodly and so she took a scissors and went around and cut all the fringes off. Cut the fringes off the lamp shades in a convent parlor without so much as asking anyone?

How could she have done that?

Come on, I said to myself, *you know how she did it.* Out of her liveliness. Out of the pure joy she found in high jinks. With the sparkling self-assurance she had in those days. Cutting the fringes came quite some time before marriage, lack of money, children, and brain cancer would test her and still not find her totally subdued.

Now I could feel myself ready to grasp the shears.

I had always loved cutting with a scissors, and paper dolls were my chief delight. Only sharp scissors would do; dull scissors literally pained me. I had hubris about the precision of my cuttings—the way I snipped around my paper-doll dresses; around the edges of a navy skirt hem or the taupe sleeves of a blouse; around the white tabs that would bend back and fasten the clothes close against the smiling cardboard dolls.

I had control of the scissors on Profession Day, February 2, 1963. I felt my thumb and forefinger slip into the two finger holes and curl around them. I took my vows of poverty, chastity, and obedience and snipped and snipped, and the garish fringes dropped away. Anything not necessary to what I thought was the life of perfection and beauty dropped away, onto the waxed and polished floors.

The Black Veil

The change from white veil to black seemed hugely sophisticated, as if we had been Kansas residents caught up into the air, hurled eastward, and transformed into full-fledged New Yorkers in the space of twenty minutes.

It felt all over again like growing up, like all my graduations combined. In addition, it symbolized my new life with Christ.

It set us completely apart from the novices, who looked at us, the newly professed, admiringly. It bound me more closely to my set. We all looked older, wiser. And we knew we had all made it through boot camp.

I looked, I thought, even more like Jackie Kennedy now, because I had the black veil. Jackie Kennedy had dark hair. A black veil went nicely with dark eyes and— *Stop* that line of thinking, I said, interrupting myself, *right now. Quit it.*

Sister M. assumed the position of our new superior. She moved quickly, was sensible, kind, smart, expressive, jolly at times. She looked healthy; she had flushed cheeks as if happiness lay upon her. She taught Spanish. Was it perhaps a more lively language than French? My father used to say that a person living in this hemisphere should study Spanish—it was only common sense. Maybe, I thought, I should have taken his advice.

A measured but deep affection is what she inspired. Along with receiving the black veil, along with making vows, this new superior's vital and generous demeanor made me almost dizzy with good cheer. Sister M. would have made a wonderful mother.

And there was even more in which to rejoice. We were to return to Clarke College, a short daily bus ride across Dubuque, as professed Sisters in order to continue our college educations. Clarke College had been *my* college for a year. I was going back.

Back to School

In the course of the spring 1963 semester and the following summer semester, I took modern European history, Biology I and II, parts I and II of a survey of English literature, Far East history, and modern drama.

We were in awe of the quality of the teaching. In only one class did the professor seem odd and difficult; she was patronizing to us, to the freshly vowed faces that we were.

The Clarke laywomen groaned when we started classes spring semester. Young nuns who were mostly smart and studied like crazy kept everyone else who wished to compete academically in harness all the time.

Studying was the Will of God for nuns, and the college women watched the Sisters take notes, underline, show up each day for class, read everything, review their notes, make up study guides for one another, set study session appointments. The way they paid attention to what the professor said was scary. They had superb handwriting and were demon spellers.

The nuns did not have to deal with boyfriends or with parents, worry about money, set their hair in rollers, drink too much, run out of cigarettes, think about careers, spend time on the telephone, go out on Friday and Saturday nights, drive cars, go home for long vacations, go shopping.

As for us, the nuns, the classes were a little complicated. Pride in an apt contribution in class, pride in excellent grades, pride in any form was a thing to be subdued. We did not let others see our grades. Many a test paper with a 98 on it was folded vertically and spirited out of sight. In class discussion, many of us couched our answers so as not to appear too sure of ourselves.

I was positive that no one would ask me to fail an exam as the superior had all but asked Sister Luke to do when she was facing her tropical medicine orals. What a relief to think I didn't have to struggle with that.

Excelling in our studies, of course, meant the community would profit; it would have more and better teachers. Some in my set would go on for advanced degrees, which would also be of value to the work, largely teaching, of the BVMs.

Like a Buddhist

My superiors and I agreed that my major would be English and my minors philosophy/theology, education, library science, and history. My Far East course at Clarke was taught by Sister Q., a brilliant woman and veteran teacher.

My favorite part of the course was the China segment. Here I learned about Matteo Ricci, the Italian Jesuit who left Macao disguised as a Buddhist and ventured into mainland China. He wanted to bring Christianity to China and he wanted to do it in such a way that he did not discredit or appear to discredit Buddhism or Taoism or Confucianism.

I admired him. I admired his superiors. They let him *do* that? They let him and his companion dress up as Buddhists? They did. I learned that this cultural sensitivity was often characteristic of the Jesuits.

For the first time, in 1963, I saw other religions as things one could heartily respect.

And China—the *things* there were to learn about it.

China contained blue-and-white porcelain; pelicans on loose, long leashes getting fish for the Chinese people; gourd cricket cages; worms bred to spin silk in the trees. Chinese raw materials and Chinese objects and Chinese science surpassed in sheer density of imagery anything I had ever read about before.

China had grapevines and lamb, oil of sesame and palm. It had teas and cinnamon and unshod horses, rhubarb and lacquer and ginger. Fish choked the Yellow and Yangtze Rivers. China had moats and bridges and exceptional precision instruments—clocks and astronomical devices. It had bamboo and dragon thrones and cedar trees and vermilion coral and ivory. The Gobi was in China and the Great Wall and part of the Silk Road.

I got to the class early each day, poised to hear what the scholarly and witty Sister Q. would have to say. I was always reading, taking notes, darting into the material.

And I was asking lots of questions, which was something new for me. Half the time, I felt as if I had a fever.

I think I almost forgot that I was a nun.

Chicago

When summer session ended, almost all of us left Dubuque and went to Chicago, where we would continue to work on our B.A.'s at the community's other college: Mundelein.

Chicago was the Carl Sandburg of my high school poetry; it was to the London House that I had gone with my freshman roommate and her parents and listened to swing music while having a legal drink. Chicago was the Pump Room (how exciting—did you wear pumps there?), and it was Lake Michigan and the wind, and it was skyscrapers and the excitement of being forty or fifty miles out and being able to get all those stations on the car radio.

And it was being in grade school and vacationing, taking the lake drive down through Winnetka and River Forest with our parents, my sister and I putting our books—*Wuthering Heights, Northwest Passage*—aside and seeing the lake glinting on the left and the mansions and huge acreages on the right. We had left behind the Wisconsin motels, new as they were in the fifties, with their knotty-pine paneling.

We said, "Oh!" in unison when one of the mansions came into view.

"Oh."

"Ouch."

"Look at *that* house."

"Judy, look at that one."

"See those hedges?"

"What an enormous gate."

"Quick, look at that one."

"Tudor style." The house was as big as—something. The *Titanic?*

Papa, as we called him in those days, was driving; he wore a short-sleeved shirt, his elbow resting on the car window frame, his tan deepening the color of his Eastern European olive skin. We were drawing nearer and nearer to Chicago.

Chicago was a dream but still manageable, unlike my ideas of New York City, of Manhattan.

Chicago was like heaven.

And dangerous Skokie was in the vicinity.

When we were finally settled in our Chicago-area motel one Sunday, my father had explained about Skokie and Al Capone. The word, the name Skokie itself, sounded slangy to me, a word cut short, truncated, and ominous.

When Papa finished his stories of perils tinged with glamour, he paused. Then he announced, "Now I'm just going to take a run over to Skokie, which is the only place I can get a bottle of Fleischmann's on Sunday. Then Mama and I can have a drink here in the room before dinner. Everywhere else is dry today."

I could see Al Capone's face, his jowls, the hat that looked just like the hat that my father wore to work. Papa was really going right into Skokie to buy whiskey. Al Capone was long dead, but I feared for Papa and I half wanted to go with him.

Like a Courthouse

Mundelein College was on Sheridan Road where it dead-ended at Lake Michigan. If you wanted to go to the Loop from there, you would turn right onto Lake Shore Drive.

Mundelein was the Art Deco "skyscraper college," fifteen floors or so. It felt different from any college I have ever stepped into, and I liked that.

It smelled, especially on the first floor as I would walk in from the outside, like a big city. Wind got in there and car exhaust and some dust. It felt worldly and businesslike, like a—what? I finally discovered that it reminded me of a courthouse. That's it: it reminded me of the imposing Saint Paul courthouse that I had toured when I was young.

The scholasticate, the residence for young BVMs working on their B.A.'s, lay right across the street from the college. Here each Sister had her own room, in which was a bed and a desk and chair as well as a built-in dresser with a mirror above it and a light. There was a small closet. Each room had a window. My window looked out, not at Mundelein or at the lake, but at a modest neighborhood: I could look down from the seventh floor and see backyards, white shirts and nightgowns and underwear and sheets pinned to clotheslines.

After three years, I had privacy again. I could decide when to open a window in my room. I could decide whether or not to turn on the light in the recessed area above the drawers.

I tried my new light. *Click.* On it went. *Click.* Off went the light under its frosted glass shade.

Click: on went the light.

Click, and *click.* I didn't have to be concerned about anyone else's caring whether or not the light was on.

Click. I was controlling something according to my desires. I was as powerful as a three-year-old.

I wondered who had invented the light switch anyway.

Had he or she consulted the Pope? Was the inventor Protestant?

Was the light switch secular? But it was such a marvel. Amazing, that it had nothing to do with the Church. The Church could not order it around; the Church could not disassemble it.

Pajama Legs

For P.E. class at Mundelein, we took swimming. We swam in the college swimming pool at night. We wore regular P.E. black bathing suits.

I had never thought of nuns swimming. Sister Luke did not swim, nor did any of her Belgian counterparts. I didn't especially want to look at my Sisters' bodies. At least I didn't have to see the butchered crew cuts because we all wore swimming caps.

We were told that we might wear our pajamas under our habits when we went over to the college at night so we would not, I supposed, have to spend so much time taking off long black stockings and underclothes and putting on long black stockings and underclothes.

There we went, groups of young nuns crossing Sheridan Road with the green light in the evening. It was wintertime and dark and we were crossing in front of cars and cars and more cars. We were in the cars' headlights.

And it struck me as funny. What if the people saw the bottoms of our pajama legs—even though we had rolled them up precisely so this would not happen—under our habits?

Wouldn't that be hilarious? Wouldn't it? While driving home from work, some man, say, might see a nun's pajama legs under her habit.

Even as this same man was shrugging off his coat after he got home, he would say to his wife, "Hey, do you know what I saw?"

You think about this for a while and then you begin to think your sense of humor, although developing somewhat, has gone a little askew. Perhaps you've been too long in the convent. Could the Chicago drivers care less?

A Pear

I signed up for creative writing class with someone named Jeffry Spencer. This professor, Jeffry or no, happened to be a woman.

Professor Spencer was lean and witty and youngish and smart, very smart, but not pretentious. Never in my life had I known anyone who was a relatively young married woman (mid-thirties, I guessed) and mother of three children and at the same time a professor. I heard that her husband, David, was also a professor, who taught at Loyola University.

Professor Jeffry Spencer had a career: she was an intellectual and a teacher and was energetic and had a husband and these children (*why*, exactly? I wondered), and lived in sophisticated Chicago. It was 1963. A curious state of affairs.

I had begun to make friends with a lay student (was it still a particular friendship if I had it with someone who wasn't a nun?), a funny, cocky, cigarette-smoking woman my age who said to me: "Listen, I got invited to the Spencers' apartment: it's huge and has lots of dark wood and bookshelves everywhere and books and books and books. Sister, it's a real, honest-to-God intellectual's apartment."

It was a little racy of her, I thought, to use the expression "honest to God" in front of me, but I could see the apartment in my mind. It *was* an intellectual's apartment.

In Jeffry Spencer's creative writing class, I wrote short stories and poems. Professor Spencer was a fine teacher. She read and commented on my work. One day she told me that I was "a poet." No one had ever been so direct with me about the impression my writing made on her.

Professor Spencer appreciated things. Apropos of some discussion we were having in class, she described a pear on a windowsill in her kitchen at home. The idea as she described it was that the particular pear was just at this point in time not only ripe but perfectly ripe, or rather, ripe in some perfect way. It was a kind of Platonic ideal of a pear.

I imagined I saw the pear and its woody brown stem and I saw the light lime color of its skin and the pink blush that lay on it in one area. The pear in its colors looked like ying and yang. Or it looked a little like the continent of Africa, the pinkish part curving out like a cast net, bulging to the left against the green sea.

There that extraordinary fruit was, in—of all places—a perfectly domestic setting, a secular setting. The pear lay tipped on one side on a windowsill in a kitchen in an apartment where not only intellectuals lived but a little family lived.

I could not forget this pear.

From the Lake

I wrote, in Jeffry Spencer's class, where we had discussed modern forms of art, a poem called "The Formal Circle." The twelve-tone scale appeared in this poem and Kandinsky was in it.

By this time two of us, Sister A. and I, had been given permission to work on staff with the young laywomen on the *Mundelein Review,* the Mundelein College literary magazine. We were also allowed to submit our work for consideration for publication.

The editors wanted to print "The Formal Circle." I thought this would be acceptable to my superiors, as another young Sister's poem had earlier been published in the magazine. *Just don't be prideful about it,* I told myself. *He must increase, I must decrease.*

My superior, frowning, made some comment about the poem after it was published; she did not seem pleased. She said she could not understand it. Did I get a sense that she wanted to discuss it? No.

What was it they couldn't understand? My first instincts then were that they disapproved of this "singularity," this "standing out" on the part of a young nun.

It could well have been just that. But the poem, not really a good poem, could fairly be said to be a shade, just a shade, obscure.

Here was something new, something I had not run up against before with these largely smart women superiors. One of them had not understood what I had written well enough to talk to me about it. Furthermore, she did not want to pursue the subject.

For the first time, I was not crushed by disapproval on the part of a superior. After all, the trained staff of the *Mundelein*

Review had wanted to publish my poem. They had not thought it impenetrable.

My superior, on the other hand, was confused by my poem. In the Great Chain of Being, there was no room for confusion, was there? A confused superior was a baffling thing.

I think I secretly liked this state of affairs. For the first time I had done something bordering on what my superior thought was "not quite right," and I was half-consciously enjoying it. Was I growing bolder? From where had this change come?

Had it come from going to the skyscraper college in the big city, the city of winds, the big Chicago? Being, living, right on the big Lake Michigan?

All that unrestrained water when I walked down to the college's seawall reminded me of an ocean. Like Gurov at the sea's edge in Oreanda in Chekhov's story, had I sensed in nature "the stream of life on our planet, and of its never-ceasing movement towards perfection"? Amazing that someone like Chekhov could intuit all this outside of the convent, outside of an orthodox view of things.

Was it being with young laywomen like my new friend, Diane? Seeing Jeffry Spencer several times a week?

Jeffry was singularly independent-minded. Was Jeffry a walking Lake Michigan? Was she as capacious as a courthouse?

The Elephant's Dog

My father called the scholasticate to say that Mother was in the hospital again. He said that she grew listless and stayed in bed a great deal until one night he became so worried that he called an ambulance.

Called an ambulance?

Her brain cancer had recurred.

Mother had become dehydrated, he said. He said, "I don't know what to think."

This reminded me of the promise Sister Y. had made to me that I could go home at some future date to visit my mother. I had asked her about it once, but she had been so discouraging I had not pushed it.

Because this hospitalization forced me to feel something, I reached way down in spite of myself, and at the bottom lay anger. No, I said to myself, get rid of that, you mustn't entertain anger.

But I did ask to go home and I did get permission.

Sister O.—sweet, pale, cheerful, elderly—was my companion. On the train, people deferred to us: we were in the Middle West, after all; we were sailing through Wisconsin, where people gave up their seats for the clergy, venerated the clergy. Am I clergy? I wondered. Yes, I said to myself, you are.

People looked at us. I did feel venerated. Did they know how young I was? Did I still look young? Probably.

All the daydreaming, before I would catch myself, that I had done about eating in the dining car came to nothing on this trip. We were not traveling during the noon hour.

In the Saint Paul depot, when my father saw Sister O. and me coming, he took off his hat. He hugged me and Sister O. said simply to him, "Here's Sister Mary Deborah's *father*," with empathy.

My mother cried when she saw me enter her hospital room with my father. Sister O. had stayed back at the convent. Mother in crying made a sound similar to sounds I once heard her make after she had had several teeth pulled on the same day. After she cried, she did not cry again until I left to go back to Chicago.

I sat next to her bed. She was so thin that when she lay on her side, her hip made a narrow ridge in the hospital bedspread.

She was mostly herself with this exception: the right words

escaped her. Because of the pressure of a growing malignant tumor in her brain, the right words escaped the woman who had such a rich vocabulary, who was a sterling speller, who taught Latin and English. The saving grace was that she did not often notice that her phrases sometimes made little sense.

A friend of the family's, a woman who had a beloved horse, came to the hospital to visit one day. My mother asked about it. Or tried to ask about it. "How"—she was struggling—"how is your . . . elephant's dog?"

My father, also in the room, and I both took steps backward as if someone had whisked balloons out of nowhere and had thrust them in our faces.

Elephant's dog? The best she could do for horse.

Another day, I came in and found her out of bed and in her little private room's bath. She had pulled a chair up to the cracked sink: she was washing her hair. No surgery this time; no radiation. The tumor was inoperable. She had not lost her naturally curly salt-and-pepper hair.

Weak as she was, she was definitely not supposed to be out of bed.

"Mother."

"I'm washing my hair."

"But, Mother—"

"Never mind. My hair needed washing."

When I left her hospital room her hair was dry. She was content.

Why had I not in my life invented more prayers, composed more original prayers? A prayer arising from her example could have been "Lord, that I may have the strength under great duress to inquire about someone else's interests even if I must fumble the words and say, '*You* know, your elephant's dog.'" And "Lord, that I may find the strength to get up out of my bed when I am dying and wash my hair so I will look clean and presentable for myself and others."

After I made up the prayer it came to me that I had given up for all practical purposes my *own* hair, also naturally curly, which my mother had prized.

How did mothers feel when they couldn't even see their own daughters' hair anymore?

Goofy

Back at the college, I absorbed myself in my work even more than usual. I didn't want to think much about my mother still stuck in her hospital bed.

I was the only nun in Dr. Andriessen's class. Tall and exceedingly thin, he was intense and had a flair for teaching: one time he slammed a door to make a point and another time he leapt to the top of his desk. The young women were galvanized. I thought he was inspired. He had opinions. He was perhaps thirty. Someone had said that she heard he was engaged, which I thought was nice.

When Dr. Andriessen handed me back the first analytical paper I had written—on Turgenev—for his class, I noticed that next to the grade, which was A+, there was a long commentary from him, written in a bold hand.

Good, I thought. I had always loved commentaries from my professors and I was eager to see what this one said.

What the note said was that my paper was marvelous and that it was of professional caliber and that he thought it could be published and that he was willing to help me get it published and that he wished I would come to see him in his office.

Good grief.

Praise again. What to do with it? My face felt warm.

A professor had asked me to come to see him. A professor had asked me to come to his office. Of course, the thing to do was to settle myself down and go to see him.

The conference consisted of his saying over and over again how much he admired the paper. I noticed that he was restless, which was consistent with his flamboyant behavior in our class. The idea of publishing did not make much sense to me for I knew a thing or two: in other classes I had been assigned to read articles from the journal *PMLA* and my own critical essay sounded far less scholarly by comparison. What I had written was more dilute, more eccentric.

The time came when members of our course were to give oral reports. As this was going on one day and as I was taking notes, Dr. Andriessen came and sat in the vacant row behind me. And in the seat directly behind mine.

I could feel that he had put his feet up on the lowest rung of my chair because it shuddered slightly. He must have been moving his feet, wiggling the chair.

What kind of man would put his feet up on the rung of a chair that some nun was sitting in and then jiggle it? At the same time, an alarming smell came to me: alcohol. Had he been drinking? But that would explain his feet on the chair—the alcohol was making him feel uninhibited. I decided he had been drinking and that now he was acting goofy.

He acted goofy like the boys I knew in seventh grade, who talked, twitched, and wondered what to do with the girls and with their own lengthening legs under the desk. They were the boys whom Sister called "Mr. Man."

"Sit down, Mr. Man."

"Don't put your feet on the chair, Mr. Man."

To a boy named Eugene, Sister said, "You smell like tobacco, Mr. Man. Don't you know that smoking will stunt your growth?"

Eugene was the tallest seventh-grader I had ever seen.

What was worse? Alcohol, or garlic?

Dr. Fortunati's breath had bothered Sister Luke (who was fasting before Mass) during the morning surgeries; it smelled of garlic. She had eventually made some comment to him about it and he had laughed and said, shockingly, that Madame Lamartine—who was his mistress—complained to him about the same thing. But Dr. Fortunati had stopped eating garlic for Sister Luke's sake—so that she would not get nauseated while she assisted him at the operating table.

Would Dr. Andriessen have given up drinking and rattling my chair so that I would be comfortable? The difference was that I would not have spoken to Dr. Andriessen about his breath or about his jiggling.

A Call

"Sister," one of my superiors said, "he sounded as if he might be intoxicated."

After evening prayers, Sister B. had caught my eye at the door of the chapel and asked if she might speak to me. I thought it was strange because we were all making a retreat, and also the hour of the Grand Silence was approaching.

Dr. Andriessen had just called the convent and asked, if not demanded, to speak to me. I was incredulous. He knew better than to call up a young nun, his student, on the telephone, at a convent at night.

Sister B. had told him that I was on retreat. She and I whispered together about my professor's odd behavior. She was as taken aback as I was but, as always, this particular superior was sensible and sympathetic.

"Do you think," she said, "you might have done anything to encourage him, Sister?"

The knee-jerk reaction would have been hurt feelings—my usual hypersensitivity to anything that suggested criticism of me. This woman, however, was so good and felt so trustworthy that the question didn't bother me.

"No, Sister." I told her about the paper of mine on which Dr. Andriessen wrote the lengthy note and I offered to show it to her. She took me up on the offer.

She suggested that I keep a good distance from him. Which, I said, of course, naturally, absolutely, I would do.

You feel flustered.

Flush.

Blush.

In blushing, vasodilation occurs. The skin flushes, reddens. Heat can cause this and so can emotion.

But as a young Catholic woman you had mostly learned to banish the advent of an emotion or an emotion itself, whatever it was, before you even knew what it was about, before you could examine it and learn about yourself or follow its lead or cut yourself some slack. The more quickly you got rid of it, the less likely it would be a sin, a spot on your soul.

I was flushed over Dr. Andriessen's behavior.

And I didn't want it. I wanted to ditch it. This unwonted, unwanted flushing.

"But yet," says John Donne, "the body is [the] booke."

Although all this attention upset me, it also made me feel special: I must not be identical to the nun next to me because my teacher wasn't chasing anybody else; he was chasing *me*. This feeling was another occasion for guilt, of course, for the life I had chosen had nothing to do with being singled out, with being noticed—there were to be no heavy treadings, no sprawlings, no flyings up or dartings out. I had been taught to keep it down, be modest, hold it in, sacrifice, stand back, fit in, serve, and be humble.

I could not quite understand, though, why he was doing this. Since I was swathed in black, he couldn't really tell what I looked like. Men were supposed to be attracted to women's bodies.

Then I thought of my paper on Turgenev. Could it be that men acted goofy, drank, and then pursued women because of their *minds*?

More likely it was the Jackie Kennedy thing again.

I would avoid him. I would use custody of the eyes.

The first thing that happened when I went over to the college after our retreat was that I ran directly into him.

He stopped right in front of me and said, sarcastically, "I thought you were on *retreat*."

Which brought me to the reality of his call. It had not been a dream. He had telephoned the convent, wanting to speak to me at night. Even Dr. Fortunati would not have done such a thing.

Professor Andriessen had to be crazy, I decided, to be so bold. The man was insane.

"I was," I said. "But now it has ended."

He walked away. To my relief.

The class ended. I didn't see Professor Andriessen again. I realized, to my dismay, that I was disappointed.

His Marble Jaws

One of the younger Sisters, Sister F., whom I did not know very well—whom *did* I know well?—became ill during our time together. About all I knew was that the disease was serious.

How could this have been? I had thought of nuns, except the very old nuns, as invulnerable and invincible. A nun was sick? A young nun was sick? How odd, how peculiar. Someone who wanted to serve God was sick?

Sister F. had been hospitalized; we took turns visiting her. The day I was assigned to go, the superior who accompanied us said we would not stay long in her room—we would just stop in and say hello. Say "sorry." We were sorry that she was ill and we were all praying for her.

Sister F. did not especially want to say hello. Sister F. was practically incapable of saying hello. There were several nurses at her bedside and I could not really get a clear, full view of her.

But we saw enough. We saw that she lay in her nightgown and her nightcap in the immaculate bed with the side rails up as if she were an infant.

I felt a sense of dim shock at the mere sight of a nun in bed. Since we were not allowed to visit one another's bedrooms, I had never, though I had lived in the convent for two years or so, ever seen another nun lying in bed.

In the fetal position, Sister F. lay on her side. Her body looked stiff, as if she were in the throes of rigor mortis. And her hands looked even stiffer, more unnatural than those of a dead person might look. This was because her fingers were peculiarly bent as if they were fern fronds, as if they had frozen in the act of playing the piano or typing a letter. Pain was twisting her.

These things were not supposed to happen to nuns. Not to nuns and not to pretty nuns. Sister F. was pretty.

In the next weeks I tried to ignore the vision of Sister F. in her sterile bed. And then one day I saw a nun from some distance walking down the stairs.

Sister F.

"In remission," someone said.

Up walking around after the shape she had been in when I saw her in that giant crib? What was more terrible: seeing her helpless in that bed, or seeing her risen, up walking again, up waiting for the next recurrence?

It was worse than seeing Hamlet's father's ghost: "Tell why," Hamlet said,

> the sepulcher
> Wherein we saw thee quietly inured
> Hath oped his ponderous and marble jaws
> To cast thee up again.

It was worse than my first sight of the sketch of Marley's face—a cloth tied from his chin to the top of his head so as to keep his jaw from sagging—as the door knocker in my children's book of *A Christmas Carol*, the sketch someone had scribbled over (I had never scribbled—*had* I?) with purple crayon.

It was the very type of a kind of loss of control that I had entered the convent to avoid.

But wait a minute. Yes, of course, another nun in my experience had been ill. Sister Luke had been ill; Sister Luke had had TB.

A Curtain of Night Moths

But Sister Luke convalesced in a tentlike structure in the Congo, which seemed to be in the treetops, and she had an affectionate monkey for a companion, and from the crystal wineglasses she swallowed those raw egg yolks sprinkled with that parsley and lemon juice. Dr. Fortunati had waited on her.

It was all glorious: "Her circular room under the thatch was walled with fine-mesh screen which became visible only when the lights were on. Then it was a curtain of night moths beating softly from outside with huge brown velvet wings."

A curtain of night moths.

And she had completely recovered.

The Country

By the time I renewed my vows in February 1964, another year of my life—the year 1963—had passed. We had been allowed during this period to follow, on television, two news events.

John XXIII had died and Giovanni Montini had been elected, to become Pope Paul VI.

President Kennedy was shot and killed in Dallas.

I was sorry that John XXIII had died, but I had as yet no idea what a setback this would prove to be for the Roman Catholic Church in America.

The death of President Kennedy was something else. It was announced over the Mundelein College intercom while my Chaucer class was taking an exam. The professor put his head down and covered it with his hands, raising it again for a moment only to wave us away from our blue books. We looked at one another. Should we do something for him? He alarmed us, a grown man sitting there with his head down on the desk.

For the next few days we were allowed to watch television at will on the tenth floor of the scholasticate. I spent as much time there as I could, looking at the flag-draped casket, looking at the riderless horse, looking at the caissons, looking at Jacqueline Kennedy and her children.

I saw the crowds on television and I heard the reactions of people from all over the United States. For the first time I got the sense that I was part of something that the convent didn't or couldn't contain. The country seemed larger than the convent and even the Church in some odd way. I couldn't quite figure it out. How could anything be larger than the convent and the Church, to both of which I had given my life?

An Atheist

Professor Vidal, who taught a history course I was taking, caused a stir: he was rumored to be an atheist. Why in the world had Mundelein hired him? I had never heard of such a thing.

Parents all during those years were told by the Church that it was their responsibility to send their children to Catholic colleges. Part of it, I figured, had precisely to do with not exposing young minds to faithless professors. But here an atheist had fallen, had actually been placed, right among us. On top of his ungodliness, he looked like a football player, which confused me.

Atheists weren't supposed to look like football players, to look muscular and pleasant and well fed. Atheists were skinny, nervous, crabby, and balding. Atheists drank too much and wore black turtlenecks; if they were married, they dominated their wives in a subtle way—they had their wives buffaloed. Folie à deux. The wives lost their faith in God, too, or were at least afraid to bring Him up in the house.

Every time I walked into Professor Vidal's classroom, I was startled to see him standing there, as if I had expected him to have been struck by lightning in Oak Park or to have choked to death on a big chunk of steak in Evanston because of his atheism.

He was a good teacher, which also baffled me. Once I wrote a paper about Victor Hugo in his class and when I got it back there was one of those long comments on it again.

Oh no, I thought. He essentially said that it was a pleasure to read a history paper that was not perfectly dry. He did not ask me to come to his office to discuss the paper.

Was this man going to try calling me on the telephone? Sister B., though I knew she would never give up on me, might begin to wonder what it was that I was, unconsciously of course, doing.

But no. Professor Vidal did not seek me out to make a personal remark to me; neither did he try to get me on the telephone. He was just there every morning at his podium, a casual man, doing his lecturing, doing his job, and then leaving.

Could he really be an atheist? It was hard to believe.

Coffin

"It's all over now."

This was my brother's way of telling me that my mother had died. After the telephone call was over, I went to the chapel and stayed there for at least an hour, kneeling straight up: if I could not gain control over the tears themselves, at least I would not let them make me slump or sag in my pew.

She was gone from all of our sights for good. How could that be?

For the first time I felt vacancy as palpable. Loss of the dead was a living thing.

"No motion," Wordsworth had written, "has she now, no force." Thinking of my mother's body without any motion was impossibly confusing. And she had always and everywhere been forceful.

Even in her tribulations, even in her distress; through personal famines, through cobalt treatments, even through brain surgery; in her nakedness, in wigs, in dehydration, whittled down to nothing in her hospital bed, Mother was she who gets up to wash her hair in the hospital sink; she was she who tries to keep putting sentences together for the sake of others' interests.

And the other vibrant moments of her last four years? I had not been there to see them; they were lost to me.

I took the train home for the funeral. I was alone. Oddly, no Sister companion was assigned to go with me. Could no one be spared? Was it that they trusted me not to go astray because death would keep me focused? Who ever heard of a nun losing her vocation, her call by God to religious life, when she was attending a funeral?

Besides, I was not to stay at home with my father; I was to stay in the BVM convent in Saint Paul as I had done when I visited my mother in the hospital. Everything would be proper.

During the train ride, I did not go to the dining car. I could have; Sister Y. had given me money, so I could have had the experience I had so often fantasized about in the last years. But I didn't move out of my seat. I didn't wonder what people thought of a nun riding alone on the train. I didn't go to the dome car. I sat.

I sat until the train pulled into the Saint Paul depot and then I got off and entered the station. There was my thin father waiting, his hat in his hand.

At the wake at O'Halloran and Murphy's Funeral Home, I saw my mother in her coffin. She looked good.

What can you be *thinking,* thinking that? I said to myself. But she did look good: her short curly hair, her high forehead; her lips, thin now, but unmistakably hers. The rouge was subtle, much more subtle than the way she had worn it when she herself had applied it. Her nails were polished the same bright red that I remembered, but her hands were quiet, folded over a silver crucifix.

O'Halloran and Murphy's viewing room for my mother filled up with people and then it filled up some more. We were not Irish and there was no liquor there but the event began to take on the feel, the tone of an Irish wake. People visited with one another; sprays of gladiolus kept arriving. Outside, the evening was raw: the month of March in Minnesota. But inside, the viewing room grew warm.

I admired the striped couch and matching chairs in a private room set aside for our family. I had a family still, I realized: the father who liked people and told stories, the brilliant brother, the creative and competent sister.

So many people, relatives and old friends, were happy to see me that I grew almost giddy. So much talking after so much silence in my life was stimulating to the point where I began to wonder about myself.

What was it I was feeling? Was it possible that I was enjoying myself at my own mother's wake?

When I came back to the convent that night, the night before the funeral, and went to the private guest room I had been given, I saw that the bed had been turned down for me. And then I did a double take.

On the nightstand next to the bed, where a lit lamp stood, sat a wineglass filled to the top with what I assumed was white wine. Did one of the nuns pour it for me and set it there? Did that mean that bottles of wine were somewhere in the convent?

Well of course, you dummy, I thought to myself, one of your Sisters did that. She brought you a glass of wine on the night of your mother's wake.

Who else would have done this thing? No bartender had come sneaking into the convent with a glass full of white wine for me. The Virgin Mary had not appeared in my room and left a glass of white wine behind her, though that was closer to what had actually been the case.

I picked up the glass, which had been placed on a coaster, and smelled its contents. It was definitely wine. Then I set it back down.

While I undressed, I looked at the glass, which was backlit by the light from the lamp. The liquid shimmered; it looked so chaste, so pristine sitting there by itself with the lamp behind it; there was no clutter on the nightstand. Just the lamp, the coaster, and the—what did you call the part that held the wine? The globe? Just the lamp, the coaster, and the filled glass globe rising like a tulip from its thin stem.

I slipped on my nightgown and stood staring. Should I drink it?

Would I drink it? If I did, what would happen to me?

❧

It was all very well to say "Drink me," but the wise little Alice was not going to do that in a hurry.

❧

I was so tired I could barely make a decision.

I put my pillow up on end against the headboard of the bed; I got under the covers. I sat with my legs pulled up, my back against the pillow, hugging my nightgown-tented knees. A cared-for child I was, once again, as I had been when I was sick with chicken pox and my mother had put white gloves on me at night so I wouldn't scratch the lesions in my sleep and make scars.

I picked up the glass and drank. I knew better than to gulp wine. It took me a long time to finish it. It tasted good; it made me feel a little light-headed but that was all right because I was in bed. I drank it all and then I said my prayers, turned out the light, and went to sleep.

The next day the hearse and a limousine, on their way to Saint Luke's Church for the Mass on the Day of Burial, pulled up to the convent. I was to ride with my family in the black limousine directly behind the hearse. From this position, we could see my mother's coffin through the hearse's back window.

Why had they closed the coffin? There lay the stunning blow. Closed: I don't *want* it closed, was all I could think. I wanted to see her. She had looked good. I had not imagined that the padded white satin lining of the casket would come closed on her face and hands. I was glad I had not been at the funeral home to see it happen.

I felt un-nunlike, I realized. Mother entering into a state of glory was what I should be contemplating. Instead I asked myself why my father had allowed them to close the coffin.

If I wanted to touch her, I wanted to be able to *touch* her. No matter that her hands now with their loose grip on the silver crucifix were chalky and cold. That part of death I could accept.

It was just unimaginable that I could not *see* her hands anymore, that they would be lowered in that closed coffin into the ground with the rest of her.

God's Reputation

Our convent library had books, of course, but also current theological magazines and newspapers: *America, Commonweal,* the *National Catholic Reporter, Worship, Cross Currents, Theological Studies, Theology Today.*

I spent parts of almost every Saturday afternoon there, reading. Theology was changing; strange and marvelous things were happening. I read and read—articles about liturgy, about lay involvement in the Church, about ecumenism. This up-to-the-minute news supplemented the theology courses I was taking, many of which were taught by BVMs who had earned or who were working on Ph.D.'s at Marquette.

When I was young, I loved going to the movies on Saturday afternoons, and now entering the little scholasticate library felt just like walking into the movie theater. I had always found reading theology exciting, never dry. The articles were something to read, to *eat*, almost as I had chewed up quantities of Milk Duds while watching movies in the dark. I knew I would never become a professional theologian or even an amateur. I would be a plainly interested person who would sniff out lively contemporary theology.

God was presented as kindlier and kindlier in theology now. The problem of suffering was still the problem of suffering. I read multiple theories about evil in God's world, about how God could allow it, but they all seemed to fall short. Suffering would remain a mystery.

It did become clearer and clearer to me that the Presence who supports all life was a loving and not a damning one. At first the sense of that was overwhelming for I realized that I still carried with me the notion of a God who was continually judging, straining His mercy.

But now I was displacing those old fears, the old emotions that had lagged behind my conscious thinking, by doing in reverse what had been done to me in my frightening Catholic grade school. I had been fed brimstone. Now I would feed myself the opposite, an equivalent of the wonderful Milk Duds. Stuffing myself with all those articles was a good thing to do.

At the same time that God was beyond all human concepts, He was also close—Dietrich Bonhoeffer's "the beyond in our midst." I decided that meant He must be more interested in the details of our lives, more flexible, more loving, funnier, a better listener, more operative in secret ways, and more of a Sufferer when things touch our lives than we could even begin to imagine. If I kept reading and meditating along these lines, pretty soon there would be no room left for a ruthless God.

In modern theology class we had been introduced to Teilhard de Chardin, and finally copies of his *Divine Milieu,* which had recently been translated from the French, became available in our library. I could not read it fast enough.

Or slowly enough, the second, third, and fourth times through. God emerges in Teilhard's work as loving and indeed as wedded to His creation. And this all written by a Jesuit of immense sophistication who was also a scientist, a paleontologist.

I was beside myself. And there was a sentence, a sentence as part of an italicized meditation, or prayer section, in the book, in which Teilhard addresses the Lord; he says that hell is indeed mentioned as a fact in scripture, but that we are not commanded to believe that anyone is actually there, that anyone is eternally damned: *"You have forbidden me to hold with absolute certainty that any single man has been damned."* I reread that passage. So there was a possibility that no one was caught forever in those flames?

I had sat in class as the nuns told us that God does not send us to hell; we send ourselves there. That made sense. But hell hung over the heads of Catholic schoolchildren like a scimitar for many years.

You didn't want to go there. And how could you know for sure that you wouldn't? Maybe you hadn't confessed your sins correctly. Maybe— So many maybes.

There was a part of you that couldn't understand why there was a hell. Punishment for all eternity was pretty bad, especially where fire and eternal thirst were concerned. It was just too awful, especially if you had a vivid imagination. Purgatory, yes— you must have to get rid of some of your impurities before you could stand to look upon the Beatific Vision. But hell!

And now here was someone who had written what I had secretly hoped was true. It would have been too much had he just said that there was no hell, period. Abolish it—wouldn't that be too scary? Too radical? What would I do without my hell? It would be just like quitting smoking.

But what if no one was there, what if no one had been sent there? If this was the case, God's reputation soared in my eyes.

We had learned that there were incarnationalists and eschatologists. The former believed that Jesus took matter unto Himself, that matter was forever changed, made holy when the Word became flesh. Teilhard seemed to be a leader of this group.

I loved the incarnationalists. Matter and consciousness itself were moving (despite certain diminishments), as I understood it, toward an Omega Point, toward the Parousia, the complete fulfillment of heaven and earth.

In this view, what I did when I was developing my talents for myself and for others according to what I thought might be God's will would somehow last forever, into all eternity. It made a difference now; it would make a difference, maybe in ways that I could not even see, for the future. People in factories made a difference; street cleaners made a difference.

The eschatologists, the students of the last things, were largely a gloomy group. At the end of time, all our works would be washed away like the sands and seashells with the outgoing tide. Nothing mattered but purity of intention.

Forget the brick or stone family home; it was material, just a place (according to the eschatologists) for working out one's salvation. Forget the beloved backyard where flowers pushed up. It would all vanish.

Forget Hopkins's poetry—his superiors had been right—it didn't, finally, matter. All his words would be scattered; all his words would be lost in the final conflagration after the trumpet blew.

Forget science! Surely, forget suspect science and mathematics! All that work that went into architecture and engineering, into public health programs and astronomy wouldn't count in the end. All that mattered was the love of God.

My life had been dominated by the eschatologists, I decided. But now I was becoming an incarnationalist.

What would it mean, practically speaking?

The El

Our superior asked for volunteers. At Cabrini-Green, a housing project on Chicago's Near North Side, teachers of religion and catechism were needed on Saturdays. The nuns would work out of a local parish under the direction of a priest. It would mean taking the El to the project and back. I decided to volunteer.

The El was not clean but it was somehow bracing. It was fast and it shook as it shot along.

And then we were at our destination, and even though only our faces, the front part of our necks, and our hands showed, we were conspicuously white. The people on the streets were black and they were mostly men.

I got the impression that they were lounging, that they had nowhere to go. They leaned up against exterior walls and they seemed watchful. All around, the project buildings rose straight up into the air; there were some playgrounds with basketball hoops set up in them.

I had never seen such a place before. I'd heard that it had a reputation for being dangerous.

My father had gone to Skokie, which had a reputation for being dangerous, for whiskey. I could go to Cabrini-Green, then, for the love of God.

But it would not be dangerous for us nuns. We had been told that we need never be afraid in Cabrini-Green, that no one would attack us or harm us. "As nuns," an experienced priest said, "you will be left strictly alone—if only because, or mainly because, in your habits you are objects of superstition."

Superstition? I guessed that meant that the habit and its blackness lent us the air of being black cats. Very bad luck to lay one's hands on a nun?

Whatever it was, we, the nuns, the objects of superstition, felt special and full of some new kind of authority. We did not even have to be careful. We were invulnerable, invincible.

I worked, on those Saturday mornings, with young children in one of the basement rooms of a large rectory. Children: I had not been around them for years. I liked them, despite the fact that they were a little noisy and restless; they were cute and affectionate and said interesting, disarming things.

It did not take brains to figure out that memorization of the catechism was not appropriate in this setting. Instead, I told stories from the Bible.

After class was over, we went out, two by two, on home visits to the projects. There we got to meet the children's families, mostly mothers and siblings. I loved the mothers I met there; they were lively and funny, tolerant of us, warm to us. They set out cookies on plates. I felt myself needing the mothers in some odd way.

The high-rise buildings' staircases were external but covered. They smelled like urine; they were dirty and littered. We lifted our skirts to go up and down stairs, but otherwise we were undaunted.

We had no idea what we were doing. Furthermore, we had no idea what was most needed there.

The Ground of Being

A special lecture was announced for Mundelein's nun professors and administrators and for the scholastics. When the speaker was announced, some of us were so excited that we hurried down to our dining room to talk about it and drink coffee, since recreation—now that we were all busy college students—could be taken at will.

The speaker would be Paul Tillich.

Since we had studied his work in our contemporary theology classes, we were familiar with the notion of the Ground of Being, God as the ground or grounding of all that is. I loved this metaphor but I struggled with it because, like "the beyond in our midst," it required me to discard a deeply ingrained concept, that of God "out there."

In trying to grasp God as Ground, you had to do something akin to the early days of learning a stick shift. You had only driven with an automatic shift and then one new car had a manual transmission. It was so new that you kept, to your teacher's dismay, lugging the engine. You would drive the car much too slowly in third gear and it would jerk; it would hesitate and shake.

Get out of third gear; shift down to first, to where you want to be, to God as Ground, you would tell yourself. But even interpreting the jerking took time. You were used to the automatic— God out there. The Ground was a hard skill, even though you did want to master it.

The source of the Ground metaphor—a Protestant theologian— would be under a Catholic roof, speaking to us.

I was not disappointed. Paul Tillich was introduced by John McKenzie, S.J., from Loyola, who had himself spoken to us and whose scripture scholarship I admired. That day he said that at some point in the future Paul Tillich would be considered one of the great Fathers of the Church. He meant our Church, the Catholic Church; he also meant the catholic church, the universal church, which belongs to everyone. He meant faith.

Tillich's remarks were fine, penetrating, enlivening. But that introduction was what got me. The introduction had been shocking.

As a child, I had been taught either to avoid Protestants or else, if I had an opportunity, to try to convert them. I must not enter a Protestant church (in my mind, such a church was close to being the devil's workshop). I must not date a Protestant boy.

But the camel of Protestantism had been welcomed into our tents that day of the Tillich lecture by means of a Jesuit priest who threw open the flap. Or rather, the guy ropes of the tent itself had given way, the tent had blown away, and we were all outside together under the stars.

The Beast in the Belly

What was going on? In January 1965 I would begin my practice teaching at Carmel High School in Mundelein, Illinois.

I did not want to go there. Why? It was new; it was in an affluent area. I had visited there for two weeks and met my cooperating teacher.

What is the matter with me? I thought. Anyone would like to go there. Was I afraid of teaching, of being under the eye of this particular nun, of being supervised by her, of being caught out? She would see how little I knew in my field, which was English. Probably. But I was also struggling with the whole concept of obedience. From the incarnationalist point of view, many kinds of work were holy. It seemed just a step or two away from thinking that choosing one's own work would not be a bad thing. Was I sure I wanted to teach English at Carmel High School?

I escaped thinking about this by going to my favorite retreat, the scholasticate library, to read one of my favorite newspapers, the *National Catholic Reporter*. I saw that there was an article about lovemaking, about sex.

Oh.

The subtitle was "The Beast in the Belly Versus Union with the Beloved."

I thought that this sounded like quite a good subtitle. I read.

The article said, in sum, that sex can be personal, transformational, and holy.

It sounded like the incarnationalists were going to work on sex now. Sex holy? I would have to think about it.

I thought about it. But how many men would think like the man who wrote that article? Very many? Not likely.

If I were not a nun and looking to marry someone, I thought, I would find that man, that Dan Sullivan.

Maybe he was not married. And then I realized that to write about sex this way, he must have experienced it. But, of course, if he had experienced sex, then he must be married, must he not, if he was a Catholic?

I tried to imagine what Dan Sullivan looked like but finally gave it up.

I went about my classes, Mass, my meditations, and thought, union with the beloved, union with the beloved, union with the beloved. Union with a man. Versus the beast in the belly. I began to wonder: what was so special about my vow of chastity if union with a beloved human did not constitute an impoverished second best, if I could go to God through and with the other.

Wild Surmises

My doubts were back, I realized, only they were more serious this time. They weren't the genie or the Katzenjammer Kids or Dick Tracy's evil adversary.

Were my doubts back because of the notion of the holiness of sex? Partly, I thought.

I felt as if someone had whisked a veil off sex and underneath lay not just sweaty, rabbity, naked bodies but holy bodies who were sometimes naked together and sometimes not but who loved each other tenderly. I felt capable of that, of loving someone like that.

From my young womanhood in the world, I had known physical desire and the wanting to prolong it. Desire expressed in the body was exciting and always twined, in me, with romance and idealism.

I could get that back, I thought. I could have that again. My body was not very responsive, didn't feel very alive; but I decided that this was because nice young men were missing from my life and I had been taught not to fantasize about sex, the Great Impure, so I didn't. But in the right circumstances, I would be fine. The right young man would be evocative.

One of my professors at Mundelein, a Harvard Ph.D., young and not even Catholic, lived with his wife in a place called Ecumenical House. People there had separate apartments but pooled their money; they took care of one another and gave to good causes. It was a kind of poverty without the vow. Maybe I could do that! My husband and I.

My husband and I. It made me feel flushed.

We could have children, maybe. I read someplace that someone's husband always made the sign of the cross on his children's foreheads before he kissed them and sent them off to their little beds. *Laymen* out there were doing such things. Perhaps I could find one.

I would be a faithful wife in marriage. My husband, if I found him, and I could share our money with the poor.

And obedience? It didn't make sense to me anymore. The old Great Chain of Being I had forged in my mind about obedience had begun to come apart. My community knew it, too: at high levels, anxious meetings about altering the BVM Constitutions were being held.

I had had enough experience with superiors to know just how fallible some of them were. One I knew had a particular friendship, despite the rule against it, on a colossal scale with a fellow superior: did they think that the polished corridors of power down which they walked distracted us so that I—or we—didn't notice? Another superior was given to tirades. Yet another carried herself carefully, and occasionally tossed her head back to the left so that a word began occurring to me: vanity.

The notion of leaving had become palpable. Somewhere, sometime in the past two years, some young woman in my mind had found the wherewithal to lift a tapestry needle, thread it with floss, and pierce the underside of a canvas of possibilities.

But she had not done this alone.

I had not done it alone.

Who had enabled me?

The God of possibilities.

Father Hopkins, the poet? Yes. With his rose-moles, fresh-firecoals, and chestnut-falls. With all his paradoxes and spotted things.

Or that one Jesuit retreat master about a year ago who happened to be an impressively big man and funny, and made me long for solid and consistent male presences in my life? What had it *been* about the sandy-haired Father Mac, as he called himself, when he stood in our chapel and led us through *The Spiritual Exercises of Saint Ignatius* and cracked jokes at the same time? Even, in the retreat, when we contemplated the darker mysteries of the life of our Lord, Father Mac was—sunny. And he was masculine. I never quite got over the crush I had on him. A fair-haired, smart, disciplined man who joked and who was big and kind and sunny? I wanted to prolong being in the presence of such a person.

Who else had helped give me the courage to want to be a part of the larger world?

Jeffry Spencer, my creative writing teacher? Yes.

Certainly my mother, who had taken me to the Saint Paul public library every Saturday and who herself read all the time.

Teilhard de Chardin, certainly.

Paul Tillich.

How about the woman who owned the modest house that had the backyard that had the clothesline that supported the clothespin bag that had within it some clothespins? That same woman who liked the smell of outdoors on her laundry. The woman who, while a little dog barked to see such fun, set her small family's sheets and underpants to flapping on her clothesline so I could see them from the scholasticate window, where I sat studying philosophy. A woman and her little house.

Who else had enabled me?

My own community.

That was the stunning part.

The Sisters of Charity, BVM, after all, were the ones who taught me the poetry of Gerard Manley Hopkins, where nature was earthy and fiery the way I had known it in my own childhood. My community had hired Jeffry Spencer. They had hired Dr. Vidal, the atheist. They brought Paul Tillich into our tents; they purchased books like *The Divine Milieu* and shelved them in the scholasticate library. Did my superiors know that all the while they were launching me, like a rocket?

Without quite knowing it, I had become assimilated into one of the more progressive religious communities in America. My thought that the superiors were fallible, then, didn't drop from outer space like a UFO; the UFO, though many of us didn't recognize it, had been humming in our midst almost from the beginning of our postulancy in 1960. And now the very infallibility of the Pope was coming into question in liberal Catholic intellectual strongholds like Chicago.

And who else, finally, had enabled me to think about leaving, to think about changing? The Church itself, or one version of it:

those in the Church who studied as well as prayed and who, while knowing well the great tradition that in some ways enriched us all, stayed flexible. The same ones who in the spirit of Christ were bent on loving in practical ways their poor and oppressed neighbors. The same who, not always escaping fallibility themselves, would hold tightly to freedom of thought and conscience and who would speak up about these things.

Fallibility, I thought. Uncle Roman stumbling around in his bedroom in Greensboro before he went to Jemez Springs. How I had hated his stumblings, the noise he had made: *He was a priest, a man of the cloth!* "Thou art a priest forever," the Rite of Ordination proclaimed, "according to the Order of Melchizedek." *No priest should act as he had acted!*

He had given me, the dopey and idealistic teenager that I was, the creeps that summer. Embarrassing, that's what he was. Shame on his behalf had overwhelmed me.

Now I felt shame about considering leaving the convent—I would be unconsecrated if I left, and perhaps I would stumble around out there like most everyone else did.

But I sensed that this was just the beginning of what would have to be a massive personal shift. The community had done much for me, but it had no intentions of saying it was *OK, fine to leave, God bless you, fare thee well.* I would have to live with some shame.

Shame would sit on my shoulders; I would be blown back by doubts before it was over. The canvas would be tossed in the corner a couple of times.

I would have to stiffen myself, pick up the slack that had always weighed on me—my reluctance to *insist*. But I also knew that I could probably do it. I could even give a thread or a rope a yank, and watch the slack disappear.

I could insist when it came down to cases, when the jig was up, when there were stakes.

The Confessor

I liked my confessor, a Jesuit from Loyola whom I imagined dragging himself over to the scholasticate once a week to hear the nuns' confessions. He probably thought of this duty as a jail sentence.

Father Fleming seemed to be low-key. I decided I would take my chances, not being sure how he would react, and tell him I had been rethinking the question of my vocation.

The formula for confession began with "Bless me, Father, for I have sinned."

Silence on the other side of the starched linen curtain.

"My last confession was one week ago."

Silence.

"These are my sins . . ."

Silence, but a clear sense of attentiveness from the other side.

My sins usually consisted of uncharitable thoughts. But lately I had also had a few sins of anger to confess, anger at a superior when I felt she was treating us like children: we are not children anymore, I had with irritation said to myself, and then I had answered my own self, saying, *Really!?*

"For these," I ended with the formula, "and for all my sins I am heartily sorry." This meant I had finished my recital.

My sense of my confessor was that he disliked the ancient formula, which included the priest giving a penance, which had in my earlier years been something like "Say five Our Fathers and ten Hail Marys." Instead, Father Fleming would ask me to read one of the more gorgeous and encouraging psalms. I loved it.

The last part of confession consisted of my repeating aloud the formal Act of Contrition and his giving of the absolution. Then, "Go in peace," he would say.

I stayed put on my knees. I saw the shadow of his head through the linen bend closer. The penitent was not leaving?

"Father?"

"Yes?" A mild tone.

He listened. The prospect of all those other confessions waiting to be heard, of all my Sisters lined up out there in the hall, did not seem to make him impatient.

I told him I had doubts about whether or not, after all, I had a vocation to religious life. (And in saying that, I noticed that I was still using the old, abstract phrase "vocation to religious life." I wasn't able to manage "I think I might want to leave.")

He said, "Yes?" again in a kind way. He was really saying, "Continue, if you like."

Relief. And I was emboldened.

My telling then became a sort of rushed litany: I was having problems with the whole concept of obedience. I also saw consecrated virginity as problematic. I wrestled least with poverty because I figured I could manage the spirit of poverty out in the world. I was an unlikely candidate, I thought, for becoming trapped in material things.

At last I ran out of breath.

Father Fleming did not tell me to put these things out of my mind nor did he say to go to my superiors. He encouraged me to think about these things and pray about them.

Week after week I went to confession, identified myself, and then spoke of my ongoing doubts. He listened, it seemed to me, with real interest.

After my confessions, I had to face the next Sister in line. I had taken so long! Thank God for custody of the eyes. She must have realized, though she gave no sign, that I had some kind of *problem*. I felt my face turn red. Very few nuns took *this* long at confession.

I noticed that I was beginning to think of my Sisters as "the nuns."

The Window

I decided to go and speak to my superiors. I talked with one of them, Sister H., and wrote to another of them who was at the motherhouse for a few months. I wrote quite a lot about my doubts.

Sister H. listened. Then, oddly, she asked me if I had ever had a crush on her. I had had a crush on her when I was a novice, so I answered honestly, "Yes, but not anymore," with such confidence that I startled myself. Apparently I had finally realized that it was not such a bad thing to have a crush on a nun whom you held in esteem.

"Not anymore?" She put on a bit of mock horror as if I had suggested that she had fallen from grace. Was her worthiness in question?

"No."

She changed the subject to the relationship of the soul to God in religious life. I recited what I was coming to think of as my case. I explained my doubts, my growing sense that life in the world was holy and not second best.

"Look," she said. "What do you see?"

I followed her gaze, looked out the window, saw the sun of a Chicago morning, and saw one gray portion of the skyscraper college that was Mundelein.

"If you are not a consecrated nun—if you are, say, married—a window or intermediary stands between you and God as this window is between us and the sun."

I had an image of a husband as a window.

I said, "But the sun comes right through the window."

"But still," she said, "the window is between you and it. And Him."

I sighed.

She took yet another tack: "What about your writing, your poetry?"

The poetry they disliked?

"Perhaps the problem is that you haven't been able to spend enough time writing."

I knew enough to know that this was not the problem.

When I saw Sister Y., the other superior, she told me stingingly that what I had written to her was juvenile, immature. She frowned; she looked disgusted.

After years of never speaking to us of normal psychology, Sister Y. may have been at last invoking it in telling me that this was immaturity. Interestingly, she did not now appeal to the Holy Rule or my vocation or the Will of God for me.

Why did she do this? She expected a rout was imminent? She decided to point out what would shame me the most? Or did she in fact think that the pouring out I had done in my writing *was* immature?

No doubt, I had lost my restraint. In the letter I had babbled; I had gone "blah, blah, blah" about what I was thinking and feeling. The Mistress of Restraint was coming undone.

News

Nineteen sixty-four was over. I was still in the convent.

A civil rights bill had been passed, banning discrimination in voting, jobs, and public accommodations.

The *National Catholic Reporter*, the weekly newspaper, the one I had been reading like mad in the scholasticate library, had been launched.

Seven white men had been convicted of conspiracy in the

slayings of three civil rights workers who were murdered in Mississippi.

The Decree on Ecumenism had been published, in which the Roman Catholic Church took some "responsibility for the division between itself and Protestant churches and urged reunion among all Christians."

Congress had passed the Gulf of Tonkin Resolution: presidential action on Vietnam was authorized.

The Mass had been introduced in English.

The War on Poverty bill had been passed.

Twenty-two Roman Catholic Ugandan martyrs had been canonized.

The BVMs had opened a second novitiate in Los Gatos, California.

The difference was that this time, in 1964, I had known what was happening. We had newspapers; we had some television; we were in Chicago. My Sisters and I had more and more access to the world. This was good. Just at the time that I discovered that the world could be good, I was also drawing closer to news of it. I had begun to want to draw ever closer.

Call Me

In 1964 we were allowed to choose the Mass to which we would go daily—the regular early morning Mass in the convent chapel or the late afternoon Mass at Madonna della Strada, the chapel at Loyola. I begin going to the latter. Mass there was usually packed with college students, professors, nuns, other laypeople. There was a warm and lively air about it.

Father Fleming was often there, too, either saying Mass or

helping in the distribution of communion. I know what he looked like because I had seen him coming from and going into the room where he heard our confessions. On the printed program for Mass, I saw the list of officiants. "Michael S. Fleming, S.J." Michael.

Just seeing him moving briskly about the altar at Madonna della Strada lessened my growing uncertainty and panic, and for a while I felt steadied. Someone knew my problems and understood them. I was not alone.

Father Fleming seemed so solid. A solid male presence. Attractive, he was husky but not fat, and had brown hair. Intelligence informed his features. He seemed unflappable. I loved him but did not have a crush on him; I think that I had the sense to know that what we were dealing with together—my life—was far too important to be muddied up in any way.

I had never looked forward to weekly confession until now. One day in confession, he must have decided we needed more time to talk and that meant getting rid of the white linen screen between the penitent and the father confessor.

"Why don't you call me, make an appointment, and come to talk at the rectory?" he said.

"At the rectory?" Panic. How could I ever do that?

"Yes."

It seemed like an immense liberty to take, to ask my superior if I might go to talk with Father Fleming at the rectory on the Loyola University campus. Just *thinking* about asking to do something like going to talk to a priest about a crisis was daunting.

I was depressed: the old syndrome where I needed to make a decision and felt I could not. The old saw about the horse that must choose between two bales of hay and cannot and starves to death.

Push

Sister Y. frowned at my request.

What was going through her mind?

Did she wonder: Has it come to this? Am I going to lose this one? Is Deborah really going out?

Did she wonder: Has Deborah got a crush on this man, this Jesuit? Will he leave, too, and will she end up marrying him?

Did she think: These blankety-blank meddling *Jesuits*!

Sister Y. said, "Oh, I don't know, Sister." The tone was that of a harassed mother, as in, "Leave me alone. I am tired of all this foolishness."

Suddenly, I knew: I was going to push her.

Right at that time, I felt that there was an *I* there, if only an *I* in miniature. A tiny *I*. As small as Thumbelina.

Thumbelina had always been big with me. I could remember the day on which I felt she was I, or I was she.

It was a day when I was lying under a tulip in the garden.

When I was a child living in a residential district of Saint Paul, I loved bridal wreath, lilies of the valley, snow, lilacs and their leaves, thunder, fire, sticks, Dutch elm bark, and nasturtiums. I loved puddles, dead leaves, slush, grass, ice, green apples, frost, tulips, warm rains, lakes, and sun. They were what they were. I spent hours staring at these things as a cat stares with her whole body, stares with her feet and tail, stares even with her viscera and bones.

That day I saw a tall tulip in our Protestant neighbors' garden. I must have been small enough, like Thumbelina, that my head somehow fit underneath this flower. I lay flat on my back on the ground at that border made by grass and garden-plot dirt, and stared up at the bottom of the growing tulip. On the underside, there was a bluish cast—a sort of smear—across the rosy part where stem and calyx met.

As little as I was, I was already frightened by the notions of being bad and sinning and going to hell. The tulip's underside was comforting. She would never go to hell. She was herself. She was earthy; I could smell the clean earth smell. The Church could call her pagan or tainted by original sin and therefore disordered, disorganized; but she was still herself. All she had to do was look like herself and push up in spite of the dirt.

If you are capable of pushing, then a *you* is assumed; you must exist if you can push.

Maybe that was it.

There must be an identity or at least an entity; there must be a *you*.

Or was it that the *act* of pushing, your choosing, your summoning up courage, *created* the *you?*

Maybe that was it.

"Well," I said, "I would like to call Father Fleming and I would like to go to Loyola and talk with him."

I looked her in the eye and she got it. She knew I would go anyway. I felt gargantuan.

"Oh, all *right,* Sister," she said, the mother again; the bored, tired mother. The disgusted, worried mother. The defeated mother.

A Door

I was in a visiting parlor in the Jesuit rectory at Loyola, sitting across from Father Fleming without, for the first time, the confessional screen between us. The face-to-face felt odd, funny, bare, stripped down. I was aware of his humanity.

"You can just walk out the door, you know," he said rather abruptly.

This sentence, though not the first one that he had spoken to me, eclipsed anything that we said to each other that afternoon.

"I beg your pardon?"

"If you want to, you can just walk out the door. You can just, you know, open the door and walk out."

I imagined doing what he said. I imagined walking out the door.

A door was just a door. I could walk out it. If I chose.

If I did it quickly, gave the door a big push, it would be over before I thought about it.

I could push because on the other side of the door there was something I wanted to do but I couldn't think exactly what. Something.

As in any situation, after procrastinating and dawdling, cowering and denying, you thought—even if somewhat vaguely—of something you wanted to do that was so powerful that suddenly you were on your feet. Nothing slapdash, nothing manic, nothing pell-mell about this. After a slow accretion of experiences and self-questionings, you became convinced you were born to do something else, the next thing to be done. You pushed, then, and you were out the door.

. . .

Outside the door was something, not nothing. By now I could articulate why I didn't think it was good for me to live under the rule—*"the Sisters renounce"; "the Sisters are forbidden"; "the Sisters require the permission"; "they must not"*—and why I might like union with a human beloved.

But sometimes these bids for freedom, these *likes,* seemed so selfish. I couldn't imagine telling people I left because my theological worldview had changed—though that was true—and their really understanding what I was saying.

"Your *what* worldview? Give me that again?"

I wished I had some kind of clear cause.

I remembered a door from my very young womanhood, then, and the view of the street I had shared with someone—Sister Luke—who was going to walk out. When she left, after she had changed from her habit into rayon underwear, a white blouse, and a secondhand suit, she had had to press a button set into an "enameled plaque that said *Pour sortir."*

ॐ

The exit door clicked and swung open. . . .

The world was a narrow cobbled street with early morning sun slanting across it. At the far end, the street ran into a square where a corner café was opening for the day.

ॐ

A clear cause.

Why in recent years had I never imagined the scenes of Sister Luke's leaving the convent? For so she had done, had left from a convent near Belgium's Holland border.

Then I remembered the Nazis.

The Nazis were what did it, Sister Luke had thought at first. She had been so full of fury at the Nazis that she had felt she could no longer live in a convent. Hypocritical to be a nun and be so angry.

I had not dwelt on Sister Luke's leaving because from that point of view it was so improbable, so singular, out of my experience. I had not, standing outside a hospital where I nursed, seen of a sudden that puffs of white clouds were actually parachutes to which invading Germans were attached.

My superior's speeches were not interrupted by artillery fire, my confessor's remarks not drowned out by the roar of Germany-bound British bombers. My brother was not in a concentration camp just under the Arctic Circle; my father, attending to the wounded in the fields on the highway between Givet and Fumay, had not been machine-gunned by Stukas.

Sister Luke would work for the Belgian underground. Would that I could say I was going to do the same. She seemed not to think about men in her future life at all. Had she forgotten about Dr. Fortunati or versions of him, who might still have been on the outside somewhere? Apparently.

But I was leaving only because I had begun to find life, in all its parts, basically good, if mysterious, and I wanted to work for God—maybe along with a husband—right out in the world's layers, what Teilhard had called its "burning layers." (And Teilhard knew a variety of layers: the man who "never went for a walk without his geologist's hammer and naturalist's magnifying glass" was also the man who, during the 1914 war, joined as a stretcher-bearer the Eighth Regiment of Moroccan Tirailleurs.)

There was something else, though, that had underlain for Sister Luke, for Gabrielle, the very real catalyst of the Nazis. She had thought that there was something, something that went back beyond the war years.

And she had finally thought of it. The problem running

through all her struggles had been the rule of unquestioning obedience.

୧୬

My conscience asks questions, Reverend Mother.

୧୬

I had thought obedience would be a snap because I could not conceive of a conscience apart from its formation by the Church. We had been raised to listen to "the voice of conscience," which, though the Church did not actually teach this, had in many of our young minds come to be identical with the voice of the Church and with the Pope, the head of the Church on earth. I had been a smiling Charlie McCarthy and the Church the ventriloquist, throwing its own voice.

Sister Luke and I in the end were not so different. I saw that all the way back to the first days at Mount Carmel, I had mentally asked questions, and that though they were often not the penetrating ones I might have asked, they arose from a stubborn curiosity. I had gotten curiouser and curiouser.

Sister Luke and I still wanted informed consciences, not purely individualistic ones. But we had found that we were individuals before God.

Her thought had become mine: "What I do from now on is between me and God alone."

I would leave now.

The Taste of Straw

Still, I did not feel very heroic. How I wished the Belgian underground was waiting for me. Or the French resistance; I wanted nothing more than to join it.

But I was in Chicago. I was tired. I needed to tell my superiors.

Sister Y. said little, except that "since you've had doubts for so long, I'm not surprised at the outcome." She handed me over to an assistant superior who would help me with this process.

Yet another assistant superior was actually enthusiastic about my having come to a conclusion about this. "Now you won't always be under the black cloud of indecision."

She was right. I had chosen a hay bale and I could feel the straws sticking out of my mouth, a lessening of that numbness that comes after a long ordeal. Now I would have to chew and swallow.

PART FOUR

Turning to the World

Dos Cervezas

I was going; I was leaving.

Now things would happen fast. I was in a hurry.

Nothing was funny for a while, just as later in life there would be a few times when nothing was funny.

I had gotten so far. I was hanging out there. I had made a decision. The mild-mannered me grew steely.

Nobody had better look at me sideways.

Nobody had better crack a joke that had anything at all to do with me or my situation. Not that anyone would.

Though I was not supposed to tell anyone I was leaving, I did tell Jane. She swallowed her surprise and sadness and encouraged me in the decision that she knew was firm; not wanting to make things too difficult for each other, we refrained from talking about the subject during the days that followed.

Everything in my life now seemed sharply defined, stark, plain, understated, like the sentences in Hemingway's story "Hills Like White Elephants." Fewer details than usual, shorter paragraphs, adjectives and adverbs used sparingly. Simple and compound but no complex sentences. And if this had been a one-act and not a short story, I would have taken the part of the American. I would not have played the girl.

"*Dos cervezas.*" This is what I, the American, would have said, if I could have imagined it, to some waitress who stood behind a beaded curtain. That was how I felt. Clipped speech. No "please," no "thank you."

Taken Aback

I had been given permission to call my father in Saint Paul and tell him.

How would he take it?

When I told him that I was leaving the convent, there was a silence. He had not been privy to all my doubts and indecisions.

He said, "You are?"

He said, "I'm somewhat taken aback."

He said, "Are you sure that this is what you want to do?"

"Yes."

He said, "Well, well, well."

The more we talked, the more he warmed to the idea. My brother was in Florida; my sister lived in Cleveland. Since my mother died my father had quit drinking. He was lonely and I would go to Saint Paul to live with him for a while since I had no money at all and no possessions.

The fact that I had no money and no possessions did not faze me. That's the way things were supposed to be when you were a nun. Having some money and some possessions again would probably be the daunting part.

Besides, I was fortunate enough to have a father. He would help me out. People would help.

A Navy Sweater

One of the assistant superiors, Sister V., approached me and said that in a week she would take me shopping for clothes.

I wondered how we would do this. How would a nun buy lay clothes in 1965 in Marshall Field's in the heart of Chicago?

For we would be going to Marshall Field's.

In the meantime, a package arrived for me from my sister, Judy, whom my father had called about my impending departure. In the box lay a cable-knit navy cardigan sweater and a pair of black flats. She had made the sweater for me. All the cables, as all the handwork my sister did, were perfect. The flats were simple, and leather. Of course: she knew I would not be up to thin, high heels at first.

I could see her knitting in the light of the lamps in her living room in Bay Village, Ohio. She was sitting and watching television with my brother-in-law, the kindly Skip. Their cigarettes rested on opposite sides of a huge crystal ashtray, a wedding present. Their four children were asleep in wallpapered bedrooms.

Judy was quick, efficient, much more decisive than I was. No doubt that sweater would get *done* in time to send off to her sister, who was leaving the convent. Judy's care always had a practical bent: in my case, she was clothing the naked.

Not one row out of gauge, not one purled stitch where there should have been a knit. I touched the navy wool, the cables, the sleeves, the ribbed neck, the matching navy buttons, the small oval buttonholes.

The black flats fit me. How could she have known what size my feet were now? I took them off, held them up at eye level, and admired the grain, the stitching. Turning them over, I looked at the soles: they, too, were leather. I would walk out the door in them.

Really Pink

"I don't need to shop for shoes, Sister; my sister sent some."

"Do they fit you?"

"Yes, very well."

Sister V. nodded and smiled.

Then we pushed the revolving door into Marshall Field's and we were out of the wind.

There were aisles of shoes and purses and belts and scarves, followed by jewelry and cosmetics and sport clothes and men's clothes. The sheer amount of color made me take a step backward.

Sister V. and I had reviewed together what I needed to buy: nylon stockings, a dress or suit—and in the case of a suit, a blouse. The underwear I already had would do, although I needed a white slip. I also needed a coat.

That day I bought a green knit suit with gold buttons, a cream-colored long-sleeved blouse with a Peter Pan collar, a navy coat with big fabric-covered buttons, some beige nylons, and the slip.

The saleswomen at Marshall Field's in 1965 seemed to me to be the most disciplined lot in the universe. More disciplined than nuns. For not one woman raised an eyebrow, not one showed discomfiture, not one asked a question such as, "Are you buying that for your mother?" or "What size is the person for whom you are buying that?"

I went into a dressing room, alone, with green and cream-colored and navy clothing. I took off my habit and pondered the hair I had grown out to a sort of wavy pixie.

I stood there and looked at myself in my men's T-shirt and long black stockings, those underparts of the habit that I had not removed. Fleshy, I thought to myself. I looked just a little fleshy. I knew I had gained weight in the convent. Well, I could do something about it.

No time now to stand around staring, though this was the first time in five years I had looked at myself in a full-length mirror. I didn't want to keep Sister V. waiting. And all those saleswomen were out there, circling. They might lose their discipline and come to check on me, which would be a truly awful thing to have happen. One of them might suddenly appear, throw open the dressing room door, and say in a loud voice, "My word, are these clothes for *you?*" I grew afraid.

Out of nervousness, the first outfit—the green suit—seemed fine. The navy coat seemed fine. Everything was fine. I didn't waste any time.

I told Sister V. that everything was fine.

"Next, lipstick." Sister V. must have had her own mental list because we had not earlier discussed makeup at all. She was kind.

Lipstick. How would I buy lipstick?

It took me just minutes in front of a lipstick display to choose Really Pink and hold it out for purchase. "I'd like to take this, please." This time the clerk looked doubtfully at Sister V., who smiled confidently back. Then the woman took the lipstick from me: but before she turned to the cash register I thought she gave me a real *look*.

When we left Marshall Field's I was reminded of the pictures of movie stars leaving department stores with multiple packages hanging from their arms by the black silk cords that were attached to banded hatboxes.

A Work of Mercy

In those last days, I told one other person about my decision to leave the convent: Jeffry Spencer.

Jeffry was sympathetic and a little nonplussed. *"Really!"*

"Really."

I tried to explain.

This leaving the convent, I thought, is hard on other people, too, who know that finally they are going to have to see the nun out of her habit, transformed. Out in the world, if something life-changing happened to me, I might look a little haggard but at least I would look more or less like myself.

Once, on a high school senior class trip to Washington and New York, a nun chaperone who was on the train with us took off, at night, just the outer casing of her headdress, just the stiffened square box that at the time was attached to her skullcap. She was trying to sleep sitting up, as were the rest of us. Near Pittsburgh the steel mills' fires, which seemed truly satanic, lit up the dark in the train and I saw her without her starched outer shell. I wanted to turn my head. Seeing a priest in a short-sleeved summer shirt, dressed for a Church picnic, was also hard to take.

To see someone who has been in a nun's habit suddenly appear completely out of it would be even more of a shock: to see hair framing her face, to see this person with Really Pink lipstick on and with her neck, arms, and legs showing, would disorient the most blasé individual. It was something that somehow should not be, should not occur.

At this stage in our lives, we could take telephone calls without receiving permission first, and Jeffry called me on the same afternoon that I had told her I was leaving.

"How are you getting back home?"

"I'm to take the train," I said.

"How are you getting to the train?"

"Um—I don't know yet. Maybe a cab?" Maybe I would leave as I had entered.

"Why don't we take you to the train station? I would pick you up and bring you home with me, and David will"—David was her husband—"cook you Swedish pancakes for breakfast."

A husband would cook breakfast on a weekday? Maybe, if I ever married, my husband would do that.

What were Swedish pancakes?

I accepted.

The Church had a list of what it called the corporal works of mercy that included things like clothing the naked, burying the dead, and feeding the hungry—which last David would be doing by making Swedish pancakes for a departing, essentially penniless nun.

Now Thou Dost

I would be in silence, a full silence, again in my life but never would it be the place where I *belonged* with others who were doing exactly the same thing I was. The wood of the chapel, its immaculateness, its linenlike smell, the hushed noise of the fans, the sunlight through the stained glass—I would never be unselfconsciously part of that again.

The days of living with these smart, focused women; the days of living as one of them would be over. What would happen?

Now, in the chapel, I looked at them for the last time. I could see the way their veils fell and their capes, how their long skirts reached to the tops of the backs of their shoes as they knelt straight up. After evening prayers the Grand Silence would begin and I would not be able to speak to my set members, not even Jane. She would be renewing her vows the next day. She was still a nun.

These were the last few hours of my own vows of poverty, chastity, and obedience but I felt I was no longer a nun. What would it be like to not "have to," to maybe even not "want to," be poor, chaste, and obedient?

The Holy Ghost had somehow made it known to Simeon that he would not die before he saw "the Christ of the Lord." And when he did see the young Jesus, there in the temple at Jerusalem, he blessed God and said, according to scripture:

> Now thou dost dismiss thy servant, O Lord,
> according to thy word in peace;
> Because my eyes have seen thy salvation
> Which thou has prepared before the face of all peoples.

Simeon's canticle would be my canticle, but in reverse; the scene would be like watching a film of entering the temple being rewound. Instead of hurrying forward as Simeon had done, I would be hurrying away from the convent; hurrying away, not from Christ, I hoped, but from the days of absolute certainty.

It was like trying to unknit yourself. Like trying to rip or unravel, say, the sweater, the interlocking cables your sister had made. Or like trying to change fairy-tale spun gold back into flax, the stuff of the world.

How I had wanted to be a nun, how I wanted to be a good nun.

Unremarkable

But by the time I got to my room that last night, I was already gone, I think; I had thrown the knitting aside—no time now to waste ripping or contemplating ripping. I felt like someone different.

Taking off the veil for the last time didn't seem remarkable. Why *not*? I just took it off. I took it off every night when I went to bed.

One thing was certain. I was taking off the veil and slipping into my invisible Mistress of Restraint armor again. I needed to steel myself, at least until I got out the door.

I looked at myself in the mirror, at my hair. It was still pretty short, but it would do. I didn't think I would look like an escaped nun or a man. Or someone who had hair so badly cut that as my mother would say it looked like a rat chewed it—or like some pariah or other.

The Morning Papers

In the morning, there was a green suit; there was a cream-colored blouse. Here were black flats; here, a navy coat. I had practiced putting on the lipstick, scrubbing it off when I left my room, putting it on again at night, scrubbing it off once more.

It happened fast. I dressed. I decided I looked all right. I had cleaned my room. Everything I was allowed to take home, which wasn't much, was down in the trunk that I had been so proud of and that would soon be shipped to me in Saint Paul.

I heard some of my Sisters, despite the soft soles of their nuns' shoes, walking down the hall to take the elevator or the steps to the chapel, where they would renew their vows, which would expire this day. Sister V. would wait until they were all in chapel and then she would come for me so that they would not have to see me, appearing in kelly green with my legs showing, looking to some as barbarous as any antique native of Kokovoko.

What would they have said if they had known that I was going?

Would they have waved? *Good-bye, good-bye, so long, good luck?* Or, *Why are you going? Why are you doing this? Are you stepping up into the sky like Phileas Fogg and Cantinflas? Or is it the sky itself that is falling down?*

Sister V. knocked; it had to be Sister V. She was smiling at me.

"Well, good *morning!*" She did not say, "Good morning, Sister."

I smiled back. "Good morning, Sister." Now *she* is Sister and I am not Sister and will never be Sister again.

"You look so nice!" she said cheerfully. "You look lovely."

"Thank you."

"Well, we'll just walk down to my office—and sign some papers."

The papers said that I would not sue the community for any work, domestic or otherwise, I had done during my years as a BVM. I would never have done this anyway; I would never have thought of it. Signing them was a snap but I paused to see the change in my signature. I signed them as "Deborah Maertz," the first time in years that I had used my family name.

Then we were back out in the hall and then into the elevator, headed not for the first floor, where the chapel was, but for the ground floor, where the door opened out to the street.

Going into the Snow

Sister V. smiled again and bid me a warm good-bye in the reception area. She knew Jeffry Spencer would be coming to get me and she needed to get back up to the chapel; she didn't want to be gone too long. After all, this was Vow Day for her scholastics.

An elderly Sister who sat poised above the switchboard said, "Good morning." This Sister also controlled from her desk the lock on the door to the outside, to Sheridan Road.

Again, I had empathy for Jeffry, who would have to see me this way: hair, ears, cheeks in their entirety, a complete forehead, parts of legs. She would see me in color, too.

The buzzer sounded and in came Jeffry. I knew that she would say, "Well." I knew she would say I looked nice.

"Well! Good morning."

"Good morning."

"All set?"

"All set."

Then she told me how nice I looked.

"If we are not practiced in daily dying," Sister Luke thinks as she is dressing herself to leave the convent, "all this would be quite difficult to go through with."

Then the elderly Sister pressed the button and *buzz*, we had walked through the door and right out onto the sidewalk.

I had walked through the door.

Snow!

It was snowing and the wind was blowing the light snow around on the sidewalks. The swirls seemed to be pursuing one another like phantasmagoric white kittens. Sister Snow. Brother Wind.

When I was young I had played in the snow and had been almost completely happy. I had played for hours, oblivious to the bitter cold. I built igloos and more modern-looking snow houses and snow benches and snow shelves and snow stairs and long, winding snow tunnels.

I was a snow mole. I crawled around on all fours in every hollow and cavity like a snow snake. Or I swam in it like a sea serpent.

Later I would learn how much others watched and loved snow, too. I would read James Joyce's description of how it built up on the "spears of the little gate"; Hardy's noting how it turned steps into a "blanched slope."

And when it warmed up, snow would turn and run in the Goodrich Avenue gutters and I could still play with it as water. I could dam it up and sail boats in it. The snow was a magician.

A shape changer, like God.

Now I was out in it without a veil, without any vows.

What if the snow could speak. What would the snow say?

Would the snow say it had learned one thing? Would the snow say, "Do not *vow*"?

That's right; I had almost forgotten. My vows had actually expired.

I was somehow comforted. If the snow was still there, if it would come again and again each year, if the memory of it would stay and stay, I would in some way, somehow, be all right.

Swedish Pancakes

The Spencers' household confused me. There were five people, three children and two adults, moving about and talking in the kitchen early in the morning. I had the lights-camera-action sensation of watching or being in a movie. I felt self-conscious and quite apart from the ease with which they shared one another's daily lives. David was indeed cooking breakfast for me: Swedish pancakes.

When we all sat down to eat at the kitchen table, the children looked solemnly at me. Jeffry and David had prepared them. They did not ask questions.

Here I was. Sitting at a kitchen table. In a regular kitchen. With children and a mother and a father; with a little family.

The plates on that breakfast table could have been Wedgwood, the tablecloth and napkins ivory damask, the silverware Joan of Arc pattern, the sugar and creamer bone china on a plate edged with gold leaf. I didn't notice.

Pancakes were set in front of me; I did see those. And the balloonlike faces of the five people who sat with me and smiled and nodded and ate and who were not, any of them, nuns.

Union Station

David Spencer dropped me at the curb at Union Station. He needed to get back to his own office at Loyola. I decided that he also figured that from here out I could find my way on my own.

This time Union Station did not mean a weekend away from college with my roommate, nor did it mean a trip to my mother's deathbed or to her funeral. This time it meant I was leaving the convent.

I paused at the door to the vast station, the one dominated by clocks and shifting timetables. The crowds apparently did not think I looked funny or uncertain. They, all those colorful people, had not stopped moving. They had not stood and stared or winced or blinked. They were like my parents when I told them I was going into the convent.

I wish I could say that I darted into the crowd, but I was far from darting into anything. I just crossed the threshold and carefully stepped in among all those people. But the crowd had a mind of its own—it moved like a fast-running creek, faster than I had contemplated moving. And so the people carried me along, all the way down to that platform where the sets of tracks would finally divide and fan out toward the west, toward the Mississippi River, toward Saint Paul and home.

The Train Ride

I walked down a flight of steps to the tracks with my secret. No one knew that eight hours ago I had been a nun and now I was not. Who else, I thought rather grandly, in that whole station would be bearing within her a mystery like mine?

And then I saw a young woman. A pale, patrician face with the chin tilted up. Good posture. Short, light hair. A green-and-tan checked jacket and matching straight skirt. I looked again at her face, her light eyebrows and eyelashes.

I had been confused trying to put all the colorful segments of her together until I focused on that face and realized that the rest of the parts could be attached, snapped on like a jigsaw puzzle to the familiar head. The last time I had seen her she had been of a piece, clothed all in black and a little white.

It was Lydia. She must also have left.

Lydia had been in the set a year ahead of me and so had already been "missioned," as we called it, assigned to teach. She had been sent to one of the Chicago schools, which was why she was leaving now from Union Station to go home to a small town in Wisconsin.

"Lydia?"

She was having trouble placing me. I knew I should offer my name.

But what in the world was my name? A noisy discharge of steam from somewhere under the train swirled around my feet and ankles. What *was* my name?

"Deborah," I said. "Sister Mary Deborah? Deborah Maertz."

"Deborah," she said.

Now there were two of us, and what were we? Two refugees? Two escapees, two heroines, two blackguards?

Just two young women?

Twin wrecks? Twin hopefuls?

As we settled into our train car, we discovered our stories were similar in a basic way. We had toed the line, we had tried, we had not dreamt of leaving.

We had left.

We had had thoughts. We had listened to those persistent, ceaseless, internal questions.

Lydia and I sat together in the train seats, which had rectangles of white cloth attached to the headrests. We were not yet ready to relax, to put our heads back against the linen and put our feet on the footrests that could be swung down from the lower backs of the seats in front of us. We sat up straight; we had our marbles in line.

We sat like Yeats's swans in that cold, companionable streaming which for us was the snow outside the moving train's windows. We would make it out in that world. How odd we felt; how confident we felt. As if we knew something. Had we simply developed hunches that we could live in this new way?

Absurd, some would think, to think that you will flourish outside the convent because of a gravid hunch you have. *Has all,* some would ask, *your good training led to this foolishness, this optimism?*

. . .

I for one knew nothing to speak of about the stars. But the future drew me on—I had walked out into the cold night and had seen a glittering belt in an as yet unnamed constellation.

The Dining Car

Though made somewhat dreamy by what we had done that morning, we were still planners: we had not been in the convent for nothing. Noon was approaching and we decided we would get to the dining car early, before it filled up.

The train was moving fast: we held on to the backs of seats as we moved down the aisle, being careful not to touch the back of anyone's head or hair. When we got to the end of the car I gripped the handle of the heavy door and with difficulty slid it back. I was not very strong.

Between cars cold air rushed up from the necessary spacings, the chinks that allowed for the train's couplings and to some extent absorbed the shocks from its progress. I heard the clanks and the rhythmic mechanical rattle of steel in motion—wheels against tracks.

Wanting to experience this had pained me as a novice when I lay in my narrow bed at night and heard the insistent train whistle travel across the Mississippi and bounce around the high river-banks. Now there was no time to linger and savor what had become a reality because Lydia was there and we were on a mission to the wilds of the diner.

Three cars later, the train speeding now, we tried not to stumble or fall into the dining car. Our plan had worked: we were early. We had time to look around.

The solid, unremitting whiteness of that car made me blink. It was not only that the tables were draped in generous lengths of pure white cloths with matching napkins.

Windows let in the piercing light of snowy field after snowy field and made the dining car look bigger, expansive, as if the whole Wisconsin countryside were moving with us. The waiters, who were black, also looked solid and kindly and elegant; they carried menus with heavy black covers, and wore white coats and large white napkins, precisely folded, over their forearms.

The whiteness reflected from all the silver and glass in that car: weighty flatware, silver napkin rings and silver coffeepots, water goblets. Small, anchored, silver baskets kept the silver salt and pepper shakers and crystal bud vases from flying off the tables. The ashtrays looked heavy. Even our plates were white.

The vases held single yellow roses, their petals still tightly furled as if loosely twisted by someone, and sprigs of maidenhair fern. The roses rocked back and forth a bit with the motion of the train.

I saw that it was good. Someone besides the BVMs had taste, a sense of aesthetics, after all. Who was it? Who or what lay behind the design of the dining car?

We were seated at a table that was set for four; we had barely gotten our knees under the tablecloth when a waiter approached, smiling, with an elongated silver dish lined with white linen; inside were warm cloverleaf rolls. He left and came right back with a dish of butter and a delicate instrument that skewered the hard, square pats so that he could deposit them on our bread and butter plates.

We had bread and butter knives. In the convent only the visiting priests' dining room had the table laid with bread and butter knives.

Lydia and I smiled at each other and opened our menus. I touched one of the printed white sheets with my fingertips. The paper felt a little like parchment.

My fingertips. I looked down at them, at my short nails, at my forefinger resting under "Fillet of Sole," printed in a type that looked half cursive. It was the first time in a long time that I had looked so closely at my fingers.

But—and was this sad?—my fingertips were not consecrated anymore. They were just plain.

The menu was not plain, though. Indeed, the menu itself with its choices of tomato juice, shrimp cocktail, fruit cocktail, chicken croquettes, creamed peas, au gratin potatoes, and chocolate parfaits looked almost consecrated.

How would we choose? Before we had much time to think, the maître d' was looming above us.

"Would you ladies—" he said.

Ladies.

"—would you mind if I were to seat two others here at the table with you?"

The car had begun to fill. We knew about dining cars from when we had been girls riding the trains. Sharing tables was common. Oh, yes, we would be happy to share our table. It would be impolite not to do so.

Lydia was the one who could see our table companions approaching. I had my back to them.

She opened her eyes wide at me. Before I had time to say anything to her, I saw a dark green shirtsleeve out of the corner of my eye.

Our lunch partners were to be two young men, about our age.

Lydia seemed to be panicked and I thought I should be panicked, too, but improbably it struck me as funny. This redheaded young man and that dark-haired one, perfectly pleasant college students, had no idea.

It struck me as funny and it struck me as fun. Where had this rising levity in me come from all of a sudden? It wasn't like me.

When they left our table, the young men had no idea.

Lydia and I had simultaneously and wordlessly said to each

other, *No. Don't.* The four of us talked politely about courses we'd taken at college.

But it would be such a story: *See, these two young nuns, well they're not actually nuns anymore but they still feel like nuns because they just left the convent that very wintry morning in February, well they get on the train at Chicago's Union Station and toward noon they go excitedly to the dining car for lunch and the maître d' asks them can he seat two other people with them and they say why yes of course, certainly, and when the two others, they're friends, arrive at the table they are these fairly handsome-looking young men if you can believe it.*

Telling this story would be like telling a joke about a couple of unwitting men who walk into a bar and see two gorillas drinking bottles of Hamm's beer. But to whom would I tell it?

My *father,* I guess?

For I was going back to a place where I had no real friends anymore. Those who had not married had mostly fled the Minnesota cold and snow—the foot-deep car-tire ice ruts on the side streets, the frozen car batteries—for California or Oregon. I had no friends in the world.

The First Evening

My father, bone-thin, dark-skinned, wiry as ever, his wool overcoat looking much too big for him, still wore the hat that looked like Al Capone's. All the way home, driving me from the Saint Paul depot in his royal blue Plymouth, he talked. And smoked.

I had trouble concentrating and only heard bits. "Aunt Margaret . . ." The melting snow dripped from his rubbers onto the floor mats underneath the gas and brake pedals. "My business . . ."

". . . and your sister . . ."

I was unused to being in an automobile. The cigarette smoke, contained as it was in the car, curled round and round and I felt nauseated. My dad was kind, he was sweet, he was joyful finally to have his daughter back home to live with him. He did not ask me anything personal—"So *why* did you leave, again?"—and I was grateful to him.

When I walked in the door of what had been my home and would now be my home again for a while, I did not feel much. It looked smaller.

There in the living room was the same green couch I had left, the same dark coffee table; here were the armchairs and the gate-leg table inlaid with mother-of-pearl.

Here were hanging the same painting-on-silk prints showing fuchsia sunsets; my brother had brought them back from Japan along with lacquered jewelry music boxes when he left the U.S.S. *Philippine Sea* at the end of his 1950s tour with the navy.

Here was my old room with the twin beds, with the small enclosed sun porch just off it: the walls were still painted antique gold. There was my dresser. I would have to buy clothes to put in it.

"You'll need to buy yourself some clothes," my father said. "Will three hundred dollars be enough to get you started?"

I had pretty much imagined all of this, but not the $300. Would I be capable of spending $300 on clothes for myself?

The rooms of the house were growing dark. When my father and I entered the small master bedroom, he reached over and switched on the overhead light. It made the room look ghastly. We stood, looking.

The mahogany of my parents' bedroom set was the same: the bed where my dad slept, the dresser, the dressing table with the round mirror and its matching upholstered bench, the nightstands, the small lamps with their cream-colored, pleated shades. There was a crucifix on the wall.

"Now look at this," he said, opening one of the dresser drawers, "look at what I found after your mother died." When he said "your mother," I jumped.

That was it: death was the reason my mother was not here in the house, the reason the nightstand on her side of the bed bore no cold cream, no prayer leaflets bundled together with novena books by means of a rubber band.

I had not seen my mother die, though later I had sat in that black limousine and followed a hearse to Saint Paul's Resurrection Cemetery. I had not realized my mother's cold cream would be gone when I came home, that her Prayer to Saint Jude (patron of lost causes) and her Prayer to Saint Anthony (patron of lost items) holy cards would be gone.

"Look at these," my father said. In the deep dresser drawer were nightgowns wrapped in white tissue paper. They were brand-new, all different, and—I no longer had names for what the fabrics might have been. They looked silky. They had mostly scooped but not low necks; they were the cap-sleeved, the long-sleeved, the short-sleeved, and the sleeveless. Bright with color, they were magenta, blue, red, yellow. Some had lace trim. A couple of them were striped. No black ones, no white ones.

My father started to pick up one of them. I prayed he wouldn't hand it to me and he did not.

"What *are* these?" I didn't know what else to say.

"They're nightgowns. Your mother must have bought them," he said. "But she never wore them. I never saw her wear one of them." He looked at me as if I had the answer. "I can't figure it out," he said, "why she didn't wear them."

"Dad," I said, "I think I must be very tired."

After I said good night to my father, I went to what was once again my bedroom and before I sat down on the bed to cry I carefully, very quietly shut the door.

Bus Stop

When I left the convent I had finished all the work toward my B.A., except for student teaching. In the days after arriving home, I made telephone calls and found that I could fulfill the final requirement at Saint Thomas College in Saint Paul, transfer the credits back to Mundelein, and graduate. Saint Thomas was a men's college but they had been accepting a few women.

Since I had no driver's license and my father was working, I decided to take the bus to the college to begin my once-a-week student teaching seminar. On the way to the bus stop, I thought about the class.

The day was gray as only Minnesota days can be gray in February. It had warmed up a little. The remains of an earlier snow on the low grass banks in people's yards were dirty, scored and streaked with black. I did not yet have a pair of boots.

"You'll be the only girl in our class," Mr. Harris had said. "Our only girl," he repeated. It sounded like being a mascot.

It also sounded interesting, I thought. Maybe it would even be fun. No men as equals for years, and now me among all the men. And not just *any* men: college men who wanted to be teachers, men who had a purpose. What would they look like? Would they smell like anything, all of them together closed up in one room like that?

Joan of Arc had been for a time the only girl among men.

I reached the bus stop.

Would the men look at me? What would I look like to them? I wished my hair was longer and that the blond color of my youth had not darkened so decidedly. I wished I was certain about the clothes I was wearing; the dark blue coat I had gotten at Marshall Field's, the one with the big fabric-covered buttons on it, already struck me as not quite right. Weren't large fabric-encased buttons characteristic of clothes old women wore? I wished—

Stop that, I said to myself. You are supposed, in this class, to be learning how to be a good high school teacher. I had my notebook, my pen; I visualized myself in that classroom, taking notes, focusing on what Mr. Harris would be saying, doing what I should.

Then I looked down at the slush next to the base of a streetlight on the corner at which I was standing.

I looked down.

Had someone grabbed me?

I felt shock, a light current running right through the whole of my body.

All I had done was look down. I had been shocked to see slush so clearly on a Saint Paul street, on Grand Avenue, where buses lurched to their stops. Many of them ran from downtown, where the capitol building was, where the Saint Paul Cathedral was, all the way out west to the Mississippi, which marked the end of Saint Paul: halfway across the bridges, across the river, was the beginning of the wild and not-very-Catholic city of Minneapolis. Someday I might go to Minneapolis.

Here was a thick ridge of slush hinting, in its whitish gray, at transparency. There was the sidewalk pavement with the dark, indented lines that divided it into chunks, expansive squares.

There was the plain dull-greenish base of the streetlight: what was it, metal? Steel? Just before dusk, its light, the light at the top, would go on like magic, but really it would go on because of the busy scientists in this world.

Here was a curb. Who had invented the curb? I could step off it and onto the bottom step of the bus that would pull up.

I could step off a curb any which way and it would not violate the Holy Rule.

I looked up. I could look up without worrying about custody

of the eyes. Across the street were the small, dark, redbrick apartment buildings for which Grand Avenue was known. There was a bank and a drugstore.

I had twenty-dollar bills loose in my pocket because I had not yet purchased a wallet. My father had given them to me; but soon, as a result of doing my student teaching and after that as a result of teaching high school, I would make money of my own. I could decide how to make the best use of it.

It was chilly. I would be taking the warm bus toward the west, toward the river, and not to the east; to one direction, not another. I would be taking my student teaching seminar at Saint Thomas and not at Saint Catherine's because I could get started sooner.

I had chosen to be, I could manage to be, no matter how spooky this might feel, the only girl among men six days after leaving the convent. Sitting in the back of the classroom, behind the men, would be my strategy; that way I could get a good look at them. I counted on Mr. Harris not to tell what I had told him about my past.

Minute by minute I was choosing. I was putting my mittened hand out time after time to grasp the fast-moving tow rope as I had done once in high school when, time after time, to a boyfriend's dismay, I had been yanked off my feet only to end up on the ground in a dazzling, snowy tangle of skis.

I was suffering the shock of the unfettered, the dizziness of the free.

A&P

I thought I was going to the grocery store for groceries. My first time grocery shopping in years.

When I pushed the glass door open, chose a cart, and angled it into one of the aisles, I was, as my father would say, taken aback. What was this? I managed to keep moving through the store, but I put nothing in my cart at first.

I had intended to buy quite a few groceries but I left with only a large ham slice with that small round bone we used to call the "pig whistle" in place, a can of pineapple rings, and two baking potatoes.

I left with four items because I could not focus. It was a Monday afternoon and so probably normal that not one stock boy, not one produce man, not one other customer was in sight.

But every last thing in the place was somehow in motion.

The soups. The soups needed a lion tamer. They only *looked* perfectly poised in perfect stacks. They were not one bit at rest; they were themselves in motion and they were surely crowding to a fall from the edges of their shelves.

I stared not so much at their names as at the soup cans themselves, and they stared back at me. So many of them. I was used to silence: their little roars grew to sonic disturbances that made my ears ache. I was used to black and white. They were so bright red and white, so showy, that they appeared to be switching their tails. Their aluminum teeth shone.

In the next aisle lay the candy, and this time I did notice the names: the Milk Duds, the Mars bars, the Nut Goodies, the Dots, the Baby Ruths, the 7-Up Bars. The soup cans had appeared in my eyes restless. By the time I got to the orange circus peanuts and the licorice, all of the candy was beyond restless: the candy was flying from trapezes.

A Novel

A few weeks had passed and I had decided to do something about the gaps in my reading. I went to a bookstore downtown where no one would know or care who I was, and I left with a novel.

Lady Chatterley's Lover.

I was curious.

I did not show it to my father.

I began to read. Interesting to hear about the social and industrial conditions in England at the time.

I read more.

Oh my goodness.

And I read.

Well.

I read on. The gamekeeper, Mellors, was speaking to Connie, who was Lady Chatterley and now his lover. Yikes!

"Tha's got the nicest arse of anybody. It's the nicest, nicest woman's arse as is! An' ivery bit of it is woman, woman sure as nuts. Tha'rt not one o' them button-arsed lasses as should be lads, are ter! Tha's got a real soft sloping bottom on thee, as a man loves in 'is guts. It's a bottom as could hold the world up, it is!"

All the while he spoke he exquisitely stroked the rounded tail, till it seemed as if a slippery sort of fire came from it into his hands. And his finger-tips touched the two secret openings to her body, time after time, with a soft little brush of fire.

"An' if tha shits an' if tha pisses, I'm glad. I don't want a woman as couldna shit nor piss."

Connie could not help a sudden snort of astonished laughter, but he went on unmoved.

Oh my gosh.

Well, if Connie could not help laughing, I could also laugh a little. Because once you got over the shock of it, it was sort of ridiculous. Mellors went on talking, unmoved after Connie laughed. I took that to mean that D. H. Lawrence did not think what he himself had written was all that funny. I took it to mean that Mr. Lawrence in fact took himself rather seriously.

I was positive that nothing like that would ever happen to me. An American man would not, I thought, say and do things like that to me. Especially my American *husband* would not.

Especially my American *Catholic* husband would not.

Now I knew the way things could happen, though. From the novel, I had learned about some of the specific outlandish things that could happen in this world.

Better for me to know.

I would be all right.

I would be fine. I would want to wait until marriage anyway for union with the beloved. I could relax.

I had to admit, however, that I did like the John Thomas and Lady Jane names just a little bit. It made things sound more personal.

Never Seek to Tell

I had no dates, no real way to meet anyone, but I thought ahead to the time when I would. I thought about the date and the way it would go and I settled the kissing issue.

I am not, I said to myself, starstruck about kissing. Thank God for that, I also said to myself. I had been kissed by boys before I entered the convent.

No one would be allowed to kiss me on the first date, I decided. That was that. Kissing on the first date was way too fast. Kissing should mean something.

And I would know when to kiss. I didn't want to kiss just anybody even if he wanted to kiss me. Who would want to do that? When it was the right person, the barriers would come down.

The first description of a kiss that meant something to me occurred in Maureen Daly's *Seventeenth Summer*, which I had read eleven times. There the boy's—Jack's—lips were "as smooth and baby-soft as a new raspberry": this is what Angie, the main character, had thought. That sounded to me, when I was fourteen, nice.

But that was a novel. No boy in real life wants to have a girl talking about what his lips were like during a kiss, much less what anything else was like. Leave all that to D. H. Lawrence.

Boys did brag, I heard.

But I would not brag. Nor would I complain. I would not tell what any man's lips were like. I had not done so before—in high school—and I would not start now. Men's bodies and whatever I might or might not see of them would be safe with me.

Although his poem wasn't about kissing as such, I had liked William Blake's whole approach in "Never Seek to Tell Thy Love":

Never seek to tell thy love
Love that never told can be;
For the gentle wind does move,
Silently, invisibly.

The speaker in the poem had told his love and she had—in "ghastly fears"—speedily departed him. A traveler came by, presumably silent, and he, again presumably, took her. Maybe he had sighed only.

Where was that man, that one who had taken her with a sigh? That was the one I would want. A man might well take me with a sigh. Never mind the kissing at first.

Fly

When I did have my first date after leaving the convent, it was blind. Stan, a fellow schoolteacher who was engaged, had a friend who was coming in from Saint Louis: would I like to go out with this Charles? We would double with Stan and his fiancée. I liked Stan; we had often talked in the teachers' coffee room; I had earlier told him about myself.

I said yes to the date.

"And oh," Stan said, "well, Charles is not Catholic."

Well. OK.

The night Charles and I went out, the night he came to pick me up, my father greeted him and then came to my half-open bedroom door at the back of the house. "He's here," my father said quietly and a little flatly, I thought.

I couldn't resist asking, in a whisper—effectively putting my father in the position of being my girlfriend—"What does he look like?"

"Well," Dad said thoughtfully, "well, he has a pleasant and open face."

That sounded good. And he must have a brave and adventurous side to him to agree to take a former nun out on a blind date, especially when he was not Catholic. I don't think I could have done that had I been a man. This would be the first non-Catholic man I had ever gone out with. This would be my first date in six years.

I was going out with a man who was actually sitting in the living room waiting for me.

I was going out.

I brushed through my hair one last time and looked at myself in the mirror. OK.

Good enough. I was ready. A date.

"Now fly or you'll be late," a good-hearted character had said in some novel to another character who needed lots of encouraging. As I walked out the bedroom door and headed toward the living room, I pretended someone—a good-hearted God, that's who—was saying it to *me*.

"Fly! Or you'll be late!"

Epilogue

Forty Years Later

Forty years later, I live in the woods just outside Gettysburg with my husband, David, whose field is physics. I write and I teach. We prize the children we have between us: my daughter; David's son; David's second son, whom we lost to severe mental illness a few years ago.

We prize our life together. We live in faith.

And Forty Years Later

And forty years later, I undertook to write about my time in the convent; I would not have been ready to do so earlier. I contacted Mount Carmel and asked to come at a time convenient for the Sisters and work in the BVM archives, which are open to the public. I made airplane reservations to Dubuque.

I had visited there once a few years ago with David and my sister and brother-in-law; we had taken a brief tour. So, I had thought that the shock of return to the convent would be somewhat mitigated.

This time I would go alone to do work. I went in March 2003.

On the approach to Chicago on a cloudless day, our American Eagle Embraer jet flew over part of Lake Michigan. Under the sun, the dreamy ultramarine was scored by pockets or patches of ice, and when we descended lower and then lower, I saw that the patches were themselves fractured so that they looked like illustrations of the tectonic plates of continents. Then on to Dubuque we went.

On the seventeenth of March, after a night in a dreary hotel that described itself as premiere, I drove down Grandview Avenue in Dubuque and approached the entrance to Mount Carmel. No taxicab involved this time and no smoking. (Though I had started smoking again after I left the convent, I had given it up forever in 1974 after fifteen failed attempts.)

The entrance to the land on which I had lived was totally open now: townspeople walked and jogged on the convent grounds. A plain sign read, "This is holy ground," and went on to explain that Mount Carmel was a nuclear-free zone.

I was going to look hard at the river this time. In the early 1960s, the freight of what I was doing, the heft of what I supposed I was doing, got in the way of rivers and everything else. I got out of the rental car and there it was: the Mississippi, muddy this March 17, and wide. How pleased I was, unaccountably pleased that the river was still there and that I had come back in my new state to see it.

The Mount Carmel buildings themselves had a different effect on me. This time I felt a pall.

Like that woman who dreams herself back at Manderley, like Jane Eyre staring at the blasted, fire-ravaged Thornfield, I stood before the structures in which I had lived. Would the nuns who were still there have perhaps become a bit like Mrs. Danvers or Grace Poole—guarding some secret from the past, disapproving, frowning at the likes of me?

Was the convent witness now to the mortal, smoldering shell of my own youth? Was that it?

That I had not written about these years because I had been unready to give them up to prose or to anything else?

The Sisters at Mount Carmel were mostly in ordinary dress; a few chose to wear dark colors and some semblance of a veil. Many wore green that day. Of course! Saint Patrick's Day.

They knew I was coming and they welcomed me to the archives. They invited me to lunch. There was some uncertainty all around.

On my part: what will I find?

And on their part: what will she write?

I worked in the archives for three days.

When I first came to this place on the banks on these waters, the nuns were to me—for all their progressiveness—literally hooded phantoms in white and black. I wanted to join them, find out their secrets, study their Holy Rule, maybe even someday seize if not the distaff and spindle, then the helm of the novitiate pulpit-prow. I could be a Novice Mistress! I could be the Mother General! I would be *knowing*. I would be in charge.

But in the intervening years I have found that I am better suited to be that Melvillian plain sailor of old who had been assigned to sweep the decks and gaze at the water—water in all its forms.

I realized, upon my return to Mount Carmel, that the BVMs were not hooded phantoms. Now they wore mauves and greens and blues and patterned scarves. Further, they could not be seized. They were ungraspable in their individuality and distinctiveness. No amount of prying on my part, if I had cared to pry, would yield a summation of even one of the lives of these focused, smart, compassionate women.

Why had they stayed when I had left, when hundreds of us had left? Their staying, I believe, was for reasons every bit as complex and various as the reasons for leaving.

I guessed that some stayed because they thought that this was their way, freed of a family, to serve God and people most intensely. This was an expression of their selfdoms, their idioms. Maybe others stayed out of what might look like simple loyalty.

Some stayed, perhaps, out of fear—what else would they do? They had stayed too long to build a career or relationships in the world. Others stayed and quietly effected a kind of living, ideal church or community—the kind some of us would drive miles to every Sunday morning if we could.

Of course it is true that as you age as a nun, your options may be somewhat limited if you leave. What are the chances of your meeting someone with whom you could happily establish, if you wanted to, a long-term love relationship?

Who knows? What are *anyone's* chances?

But it can happen.

Back at home after doing my research I received an invitation. "Come Home," it read. The BVMs had been celebrating the two hundredth birthday of their foundress, Mary Frances Clarke, all year long. The climax was to be at the annual gathering at Mount Carmel, Dubuque, and former BVMs were invited to share in this from August 8 to 10, 2003.

I did not feel as if I were going home—my present home is in the woods with my husband—but I had said I would come and I headed back to Dubuque once again on the Embraer regional jet, which plane I have grown to love for its very smallness. Later, people told me that there may soon be no more jet service to Dubuque.

From my spot in the single-seat window aisle I did not or could not see Lake Michigan. But I knew it had changed; it contained no ice continents this time.

I did see clouds.

Clouds were everywhere in various forms—above us, below us, parallel to us. We flew between them and we flew through them.

Some of the cirrus clouds seemed serous to me: watery tissues. These were about midwindow and sometimes ran between the cumulonimbus, which looked like Everests. Or they looked like great glaciers, glaciers that slid up instead of down and all the while seemed to be coming undone. My brother-in-law, a former pilot, calls these clouds "thunder bumpers." When we flew or seemed to fly into them, we occasionally felt little jolts, little buckings or bucklings.

I also saw the Susquehanna at the beginning of my trip and, toward the end, the Mississippi. Both looked muddy and from above I saw their fish-shaped islands, green from the full-leaved states of the woods.

Jane N., Margaret M., my old friend Teresa, and I had been corresponding. We had found one another's e-mail addresses by means of a reunion of the Set of 1960 (which I had not been able to attend), three years ago at Flathead Lake in Montana.

Jane, who had come from Illinois, and Margaret, who had come from Nebraska, had previously written to say that they would pick me up at the Dubuque airport. Tessa was still en route from the West Coast. All three had left the BVMs.

Jane and Margaret had been volunteering at the mother-house, at Mount Carmel, for the past three days: they drove elderly Sisters places; they went out shopping for a dress for a Sister who couldn't leave the motherhouse; they assisted with office work. They sat out on the front lawn on a bench in the evening and had glasses of wine while Margaret smoked her evening cigarette (she smoked one a day).

I had not seen them in forty years—since I had left the convent in 1965. Their faces were the same: kind and alert, intelligent and reflective. Now, however, I saw, as they approached me, a sunny quality, an expressiveness that was new. They were not practicing custody of the eyes.

We are suddenly not in our past anymore. We are in the present, in our present together.

Jane's hair is gray, attractively styled, as is Margaret's, which is auburn. My hair is the longest of the three of us and they say, "Oh, *look* at you in *hair*! You look wonderful in hair, so pretty."

This is the beginning. When we leave Dubuque at the end of our weekend, Jane will have the last words.

"We have a future."

As Jane's Jeep carries us away from the tiny Dubuque airport, we talk. Jane, single, is retired from teaching and curriculum work.

Margaret, who left the convent several years after I did, met Ray but did not marry him for several years. This is Ray's second marriage. "Ray just *loves* me," she says simply. She loves Ray. She had become good friends with a priest when she was still in the convent. Though sexual expression was not involved, she said she thought, Oh *this* is what it's like to be with a good man, and then she thought: I'm out of here. She said good-bye to the priest forever. And then she left. Thinking of all my 1965 hand-wringing, I envy the ease with which she made her decision.

Tessa arrives, joining us at Mount Carmel. Her hair is also gray; her face is youthful—once more, I see expressiveness. She is retired from teaching and administration, lives with her partner, and also rents a houseboat, which she uses for a studio in which she paints. She will soon have a show at a gallery on the West Coast. The same intelligence, interest in things that I remember. A laugh that rolls up from the depths.

The motherhouse is open to us. We leave Margaret, who is talking with one of her friends, a present BVM.

When I go to the convent chapel in which I had spent so much time with so much ardor, I am struck at how truly gigantic the crucifix above the altar is. Set aside its merits as a work of art: as the backdrop of downstage center in those days, that crucifix must have dominated everything. Crucifixion must have seemed like the zenith, must have seemed to be the point, must have seemed to be where every last thing was headed.

We do not go into any of the Sisters' bedrooms unless we are invited, but we see the places, remodeled or not, where we ourselves had lived. We are giddy. We shamelessly use exclamation points when we talk to one another.

Tessa: "Look at that statue of Mary. I remember that statue!"

Me: "This is the bathroom I cleaned! Look—this is where I peeled all those rutabagas!"

Jane: "That's where I made the supper salads! A lot of carrot-and-raisin salads and I stirred honey into it because that's what my mother used to do."

On the second floor we find a private bathroom where Tessa was sent as a novice so she could shave her legs before she left the convent. Jane had had an inkling that Tessa was leaving us and had stood outside the bathroom door saying, "Tessa C., are you in there?"

No answer.

"C., are you *in* there?"

Nothing.

"C.!" And Tessa, petrified, trying to comply with the rules to the very end, had not responded.

During our weekend there we talk.

The Mistress of Postulants, the Mistress of Novices, the Mistress of Scholastics: they became a kind of three-headed super-ego. Even now, some of my set can hear the voices of these superiors, for good or ill. Eventually I learned to handle this interior trinity by separating the nourishing things—the wheat—from the chaff of what they had said.

Tessa remembers one of our superiors saying, "Do what you are doing." Really concentrate. Put all your energy into the thing that you have chosen to do. If you are going to do it, *do* it. This saying profited both her and me.

Several of my set remember the same Sister saying, "When it comes right down to it and you're in doubt, do the loving thing," and this has carried them through many situations. Some of us think that this was an indirect, unofficial updating of the stricter aspects of the Constitutions or the Holy Rule. Translated, it may have meant that when a fellow Sister truly needed a helping hand after the sound of the bell, you stayed to assist her.

"A question I have," I say to a group of us, "an interesting question to ask, would be, 'Why did some of us *stay?*' "

Kathy, the friend who was also from Saint Paul, is still a BVM. Over the years she has taught history at several schools, including our own old high school. Several years ago she went to Ecuador to live among the poor and teach. Now she is a "Regional," a term that has been substituted for the old "Provincial," the Sister in charge of a geographical segment of the community.

We talk over dinner and later we correspond a little through e-mail. Kathy talks about high points and low points during her life in the community, echoing the conversation some of us who are former BVMs have had during a late-night session where we have talked about our lives.

But when it comes right down to it, Kathy feels that being a BVM has been a "good fit" for her. I respect her—who would want to ask for a better answer than that?

On the first night much was made of Mary Frances Clarke's Irish roots: there was an Irish dinner; there were Irish songs and dancing. Oh, no, I thought at first. Not this Irishness again. I am not one sliver Irish and now I have no wish to be. Then I interrupt myself: Get over it. Many of them are Irish and this is their party and you are the guest.

But this time, and through the talks and programs where about five hundred of us—one hundred of us being former BVMs—sit happily and companionably on the banks of the Mississippi as the weekend progresses, I get caught up in the particular story of the order I joined as it relates to America.

Mary Frances Clarke's father was Catholic; her mother was a Quaker before she converted to Catholicism in order to marry Mr. Clarke. Mary Frances and her four companions worked and taught in Dublin but then resolved to go to Philadelphia to serve poor immigrants.

After a time in that city, they decided to move to Iowa, where they first settled in Dubuque and then on an outlying prairie. Eventually they established schools all over the Midwest, including Chicago. All the while, young women entered their ranks and became nuns.

In asking questions of the Sisters during my second stay in

Dubuque, I discovered that many of my teachers at Our Lady of Peace were originally Chicagoans.

So *that* was it.

Saint Paul, Minnesota, was in one sense a large city when I was growing up but it was also called "the largest small town in America." I just knew there was something special about many of the BVMs who taught me. I thought that "though they were nuns," they were classy, savvy, smart, witty—something I couldn't put my finger on.

They were good and sophisticated is what they were. Chicago was the poetic wheat stacker and hog butcher and train hub and educator. It was swinging and toddling and jazzy. The winds blew onto it from one of the Great Lakes.

Chicago was huge.

From my BVM teachers in distinctive but somewhat parochial Saint Paul, I took on the imprint of a larger, more complex, more tolerant, more urbane landscape.

The beauties of the Windy City fog had crept in, not on little cat feet but on the soft-shod feet of the Chicago nuns.

I see that part of what I wanted was to enlarge myself.

The daughter of what was basically the prairie wanted to be a daughter of the urbane, a daughter of Chicago; and eventually she would end up wanting to be a daughter who would not stop at anything, not even at Chicago itself.

The Tulip

My faith through the years has only grown, if by fits and starts. Today for various reasons it lies outside that version (and there are other, happier versions developing) of the institutional Roman

Catholic Church, which is dominated by certain clergymen who often hand women and men—the hungry faithful—stones instead of bread.

Robert Bolt's Thomas More (in *A Man for All Seasons*), says

God made the angels to show him splendor—as he made animals for innocence and plants for their simplicity. But Man he made to serve him wittily, in the tangle of his mind!

Faith is partly a matter of humbly applied wit.

Faith can change and develop. How mine developed through both inner and outer tangles after I left the convent is another story.

But, briefly, the God of my faith, not pantheistic, is at once transcendent and immanent. God has become for me above all a Presence. God is both She and He. I love polarities.

I also love Martin Buber's translation of God's self-description in the Hebrew Bible. Rather than "I am who I am," Buber gives us "I will be present as I will be present."

But now I realize that some sense of an informing Presence had come to me by means of the body long ago. My tulip.

I, when I was Thumbelina staring at the tulip, had somehow realized that all of nature was absolutely outside the purview of the Church and those who ran it. I knew the tulip would do its seasonal dying all right—I was not a little sentimentalist. Tulip bulbs could be damaged by armies of voles and mice. But not even the sternest elementary school teacher who taught me the same year I had mysterious stomachaches could deliver a lecture that would frighten a Dutch elm, cajole a lilac, intimidate grass, or shame the slush.

Neither could the Church forbid my beloved snow. It could not lasso it, no matter if the Pope's expertise with the rope was as good as Hopalong Cassidy's when he was up on that pale horse.

The snow of my youth was profligate, spontaneous, and unpredictable like the unspoolings and irregular rhythms of prose or like life outside the cloister. That meant there could be hazards, of course: my snowballs, which I patted and shaped and collected in one corner of a snow tunnel, could melt; snow sometimes meant blizzards.

But natural things had a huge advantage. They couldn't think; they would never reach the age of reason (which the Church told me was age seven); they didn't have free will or consciences. One glorious point of all this for the young me was that they would not be punished, would not be damned for all eternity.

They were home free and I knew it. I envied them.

Some years ago I wrote and eventually published a poem called "Thumbelina, the Tulip, the Pope." In it the Pope is kneeling on a rug and a woman is handing him back a ring (she is as stony and unmoved, I now see, as that Dickinsonian soul who shut out an emperor) because of a sudden memory she has:

> A little girl had gone outdoors,
> had lain in backyard grass,
> had seen a tulip's underside—
> the bluish at the silken base
> where stem and calyx cross.
> She watched the tremulous tulip
> put by its covered catechism—
> she watched the tulip, unconsumed,
> give freely then, like nothing
> doomed, of bread and word,
> of rod and redbird, compass, staff,
> of cambric hem, of stone-built home.

The tulip shrugged off catechisms. And then, perhaps most important, the tulip could be generous. The tulip's unfettered self extended also to objects fashioned by humans and by technology: a compass, a staff, fabric, a home where people live.

I think these encounters with the object world and with persons are gifts. We embodied minds, then, can individually and communally dream up metaphors.

George Lakoff and Mark Johnson at the very end of their *Philosophy in the Flesh* argue that the "mechanism by which spirituality becomes passionate is metaphor."

"God requires metaphor," they continue, "not only to be imagined but to be approached, exhorted, evaded, confronted, struggled with, and loved." They go on to speak of a few metaphors by which we may contemplate God, including those of Creator, Potter, Mother, Lover, and Breath.

They quote the Kabbalah, which says that all existence is God, that natural things are pervaded by divinity. Here, in Jewish mystical tradition, Lakoff and Johnson say, we find that "empathic projection onto anything or anyone is contact with God."

My tulip was pervaded: I knew it. A Presence, and one that finally extended itself.

Presence is not bent on touting its own rectitude nor on the certainty of conventional positions, nor on its own holiness. It is bent on humbly filling temporality with compassion—with the considered politics of compassion—for all things, for all people.

Presence puts a fiery bloom on the green stem of the world. A world to which I have returned.

Acknowledgments

I am grateful to Anita Therese Hayes, BVM, and the Leadership Team of the Sisters of Charity of the Blessed Virgin Mary, who welcomed me in 2003 into their Dubuque archives and assisted me in every possible manner. Their community both exists and does not exist today as it did in 1960. This progressive group of women, whom I greatly admire, has worked hard and intelligently through the years to move ahead with the nobler parts of the spirit of the times and to actively reach out to those in need.

For their support and encouragement I want to thank Jeffry Spencer, Anne and Will Lane, Leonard Goldberg, Annie Dillard, Baird Tipson, and Leah Hager Cohen. In the course of my work I consulted Stephen Quint, M.D., who is Clinical Associate Professor in Psychiatry at Georgetown University and who also works expertly in private practice in Washington with recovering Catholics; Stephen provided valuable insights into the psychology of childhood Catholic school training, and I am grateful to him.

Betsy Lerner's savvy and caring assistance made this book possible. Deborah Garrison was once again a positively powerful force in my writing life—editing as she does with respect, acumen, toughness, and a poet's sensibility.

My family, as always, was my rock: Judith and Walter Marquis, Janice Kennemer, Patrick Cowan, Aimee Larsen; and especially my husband, David Cowan.

$\mathcal{N}$otes

Author's Note

xiii Elaine Pagels, *Beyond Belief: The Secret Gospel of Thomas* (New York, 2003), 165.

Part One: Becoming a Postulant

8 All biblical quotations are drawn from the Douay-Rheims translation.

In response to a question about the use of the term "Hebrew Bible" as opposed to "Hebrew scriptures," a friend wrote in an e-mail:

Hi, Deborah— About the bible/scripture problem, I'm stumped (moreso, I add after having written what follows than before I started). I use the terms interchangeably, but probably out of laziness. When you think about it, neither really captures the sense of torah, but "path," "way," "truth" and such terms have mystical resonances that don't accord with texts that are focused on living in the world. Of course, torah doesn't really clarify much either, because it works as a shifting referent—the first five books, the whole collection, that plus all oral and written commentaries. . . .

But if I had to choose, I'd go with scriptures: it fits in with that section of the whole marked specifically as "writings" (k'tuvim), and thus is a good synecdoche. It's faithful, too, to the idea that everything in it is subject to interpretation, and perhaps to the sense that sacred texts are a problem that can never be solved. Then again, bible better captures the sense of sapher (phonetically: "safer"), Hebrew for book, which is used to label the whole (as in the phrase "sapher torah"), and which serves to label individual segments ("sapher b'reishet" for Genesis).

With that said, I still like scriptures better. But I have two more reservations, both having to do with attractions built into scripture as a term. The first is that in the theoretical and deconstructive worlds, "writing" has a certain cachet that scripture picks up on (although now that theory has shifted its gaze to the material conditions of literary production, "book" may be the more fashionable term)—there's something flattering about studying it, rather than something as authoritatively binding as a book. The other is that there's something of an ennobling Roman severity to scripture, as opposed to the Hellenic serenity of bible. But as bad as the Greeks were to the Hebrews, the Romans were a lot harsher, which would perhaps lead one back to the latter term. So perhaps the best choices are conversational (i.e. "you know, er, that uh Jewish thing, you know, that scroll with the rods"), graphic (maybe there's a macro that does a torah), a compound (biblature?), a kenning (law-hoard), or, on the model of how Shakespeare and Dante have become interchangeable with their collected works, Moses (who probably didn't write the part of Moses that tells of how he died, let alone the twenty-odd volumes that deal with life in a place to which he didn't quite get).

I always thought it was God's name that was untranslatable, and not the place where you find it!

In response to another query about the attribution for this generous response, my same friend writes that I could say, "An anonymous source, afraid of his rabbi, and aware that Yom Kippur is in the offing, points out . . ."

12 Jacob Grimm, *Grimm's Household Tales with the Author's Notes*, translated by Margaret Hunt (London, 1884), 209.

23 All references to the BVM Constitutions (1958) are courtesy of the Archives of the Sisters of Charity, BVM, Dubuque, Iowa.

25 Clothing list courtesy of the BVM Archives.

30 Louisa M. Alcott, *Little Women* (New York, 1915), 313.

30 J. D. Salinger, *Franny and Zooey* (Boston, Toronto, and London, 1961), 141.

30 Maud Hart Lovelace, *Early Candlelight* (Saint Paul, 1992), 3.

30 Grimm, *Grimm's Household Tales*, 83–84.

81 Gerard Manley Hopkins, from "The Wreck of the Deutschland," in *The Poems of Gerard Manley Hopkins*, edited by Robert Bridges (London, 1918).

Part Two: Becoming a Novice

95 Grimm, *Grimm's Household Tales*, 53.

101 I recently discovered that Saint Blaise has been compared by some to

the Slavic horse-god whose name was Vlaise. My grade school teachers would have no doubt called this sacrilegious. Also, there is a supposed fragment of a Saint Blaise bone in Cardinal Respighi's 1905 Theca B, a reliquary.

141 Joanne L. Swanson, "Ahoy, Mates," *Dollhouse Miniatures* 33, no. 7 (August 2003), 41. I changed the photocopying of a map in Ms. Swanson's directions in favor of sketching it oneself.

Part Three: Making Vows

161 Excelling academically did not mean, however, as the late Mary Griffin has pointed out in *The Courage to Choose* (Boston, 1975), that the possessor of a degree, even of a doctorate, was "more precious to the community than was the nun housekeeper." Then Ms. Griffin adds, in parentheses: "There was a funny story going around, nevertheless, about the superior who shouted to the lifeguard attempting to rescue two nuns spilled out of their canoe, 'Save *that* one. She just got her Ph.D.!' "

184 Lewis Carroll, *Alice in Wonderland,* ed. Donald J. Gray (New York, 1992), 10.

201 News events are from "Charting BVM History," in *SALT* (1984), a publication of the Sisters of Charity, BVM.

207 Kathryn Hulme, *The Nun's Story* (London, 1956), 334–35.

208 Pierre Leroy, S.J., "Teilhard de Chardin: The Man" in Teilhard de Chardin, *The Divine Milieu* (New York, 1968), 19, 22.

209 Hulme, *The Nun's Story,* 315.

Part Four: Turning to the World

219 Swedish pancakes. Now we are not so sure. I had planned at this point to share the details of what David Spencer had made: the pancakes. I was going to hand over his secret for Swedish pancakes—his recipe.

But since he cooked for me, he has died.

Jeffry now says that she remembers her husband cooking not Swedish pancakes but, for special occasions, a Swedish omelet, something light and puffy. Meg, Jeffry's daughter, remembers something about Swedish pancakes but is not sure what it is that he cooked. Both of them have taken the trouble to go through old family recipes and recipe books, to no avail. So what did he cook? We can't be certain. Whatever it was, the light and puffy egg or the denser flour of a pancake, he made me feel that I was worth cooking for, that I was still special.

Epilogue

254 Martin Buber (in *Moses: The Revelation and the Covenant*) as quoted in Marcus J. Borg, *The God We Never Knew: Beyond Dogmatic Theology to a More Contemporary Faith* (San Francisco, 1997), 35.

255 "Thumbelina, the Tulip, the Pope" first appeared in *The Hollins Critic* in February 2000.

Further Reading

I include below a few books that in recent years have been nourishing to my faith. My hope is that they might be helpful to others. This little list is far from comprehensive. These were simply books I picked up because I had a hunch I needed them for particular reasons at particular times. Their authors did not fail me.

Borg, Marcus J. *Meeting Jesus Again for the First Time: The Historical Jesus and the Heart of Contemporary Faith*. San Francisco, 1995.
———. *The God We Never Knew: Beyond Dogmatic Theology to a More Contemporary Faith*. San Francisco, 1998.
Buber, Martin. *I and Thou*. New York, 2000.
Crossan, John Dominic. *Jesus: A Revolutionary Biography*. San Francisco, 1995.
Dillard, Annie. *For the Time Being*. New York, 1999.
Harper, Ralph. *On Presence*. Philadelphia, 1991.
Pagels, Elaine. *Beyond Belief: The Secret Gospel of Thomas*. New York, 2003.
Schillebeeckx, Edward. *God Among Us: The Gospel Proclaimed*. New York, 1987.
Steiner, George. *Real Presences*. Chicago, 1989.
Teilhard de Chardin, Pierre. *The Divine Milieu*. New York, 1968.

Deborah Larsen grew up in Saint Paul, Minnesota, and currently lives in Gettysburg, Pennsylvania. She is the author of *The White,* a novel based on the life of Mary Jemison, and a collection of poetry, *Stitching Porcelain,* published in 1991. Her poems and short stories have appeared in *The Nation, The Yale Review,* and *The New Yorker,* among other publications. A former Wallace Stegner fellow, she teaches writing at Gettysburg College, where she holds the Merle S. Boyer Chair.

A NOTE ABOUT THE TYPE

This book was set in Monotype Dante, a typeface designed by Giovanni Mardersteig (1892–1977). Conceived as a private type for the Officina Bodoni in Verona, Italy, Dante was originally cut only for hand composition by Charles Malin, the famous Parisian punch cutter, between 1946 and 1952. Its first use was in an edition of Boccaccio's *Trattatello in laude di Dante* that appeared in 1954. The Monotype Corporation's version of Dante followed in 1957. Although modeled on the Aldine type used for Pietro Cardinal Bembo's treatise *De Aetna* in 1495, Dante is a thoroughly modern interpretation of the venerable face.

Composed by Creative Graphics,
Allentown, Pennsylvania
Printed and bound by R. R. Donnelley & Sons,
Harrisonburg, Virginia
Designed by Virginia Tan